It's All Upside Down

What I've learned about software
development and why it seems
opposite to everything I was taught

Paul E. McMahon

It's All Upside Down

What I've learned about software development and why it seems opposite to everything I was taught

Paul E. McMahon

ISBN 978-0-9904508-7-0

Leanpub

This is a Leanpub book. Leanpub empowers authors and publishers with the Lean Publishing process. Lean Publishing is the act of publishing an in-progress ebook using lightweight tools and many iterations to get reader feedback, pivot until you have the right book and build traction once you do.

Contents

Praise for It's All Upside Down...

"While reviewing this book, 99% of the time my feedback was either "this is exactly what I advise my clients" or "this is even better than what I've been advising". This book is full of pragmatic, insightful advice from the software process improvement trenches. Thanks Paul!"

Scott Ambler Co-author of Disciplined Agile Delivery

"Sometimes we're so heads-down focused on following a process or a so-called best practice, we don't stop to ask if it really makes sense. It's easy to forget that process maturity depends upon such organizational introspection. 'It's All Upside Down' challenges the reader to do just that. Reading this book is, well, exactly like having a coffee with a coach and bona fide subject matter expert on the practical matters of software development. Paul's conversational style makes for a comfortable read which you can tackle cover to cover or simply a story or tip at a time – and then reflect on how it informs you with respect to the challenges you confront in your own projects, helping you essentially stand on your head and see a perspective you couldn't see before – because it's all upside down."

Michael Callihan President, AEGIS.net

"... Paul gives the reader the right amount of information, at the right time, following a story-telling narrative. Very nice and super informative. I just experienced several months of consulting in 3 hours from the comfort of my chair."

John Ryskowski President, JFR Consulting, CMMI High Maturity Lead Appraiser

Paul McMahon's latest book, "It's All Upside Down", expresses in words a thought that has been tickling the back of my mind for years; how we traditionally approach development has been acceptable, but there is a better way in many cases on how to practically proceed. Paul nails it with real world scenarios and solutions such that all readers may benefit from.

Jim Convery, The Ascendancy Group, Former Director CMMI-DEV and CMMI-SVC Maturity Level 3 Organization

With this book, Paul has made a significant contribution that should be of great value to practicing software engineers and developers alike. It recognizes the reality that such teams of practitioners behave as self-organising, complex adaptive systems, guided by fundamental principles, but applied in situationally appropriate ways. Insyte's Complex Adaptive Situational Model (CASM) investigates a similar reality and It's All Upside Down will be used to bring clarity to the software engineering band of feasibility that stretches from the traditional, Controlled Quality approach to the agility of Crafted Quality.

AJB (Barry) Myburgh Founder: Insyte Information Systems Engineering (Pty) Ltd., Johannesburg, South Africa.

"There are few things as useful as a variety of perspectives on any given topic. This book does an outstanding job of showing non-traditional perspectives in areas where "herd thinking" and attitudes have excessively narrowed viewpoints. Supported by personal, highly interesting, true stories, the rationale for each of the "upside down" concepts is made clear, and recommendations are made for practical alternative thinking and action. This book should be a companion piece to any traditional-thinking books relating to software management, process improvement, or organizational change. It will reliably balance out, through unintuitive and unexpected additional perspectives, the mainstream concepts in traditional work, and substantially improve the likely success of your efforts."

Richard Bechtold, PhD, President, Abridge Technology Certified CMMI Lead Appraiser

Acknowledgements

I thank the following people for reviewing and commenting on the multiple draft versions of this book: Scott Ambler, Dr. Richard Bechtold, Michael T. Callihan, Jim Convery, Bill Fox, Dr. Ivar Jacobson, Jan McMahon, Winifred Menezes, Barry Myburgh, and John Ryskowski.

Introduction

I have been involved in the software business for over 40 years and during this time my views on how to help software teams succeed has evolved so much that what I recommend to many clients today often seems completely opposite to the fundamentals many of us were taught. By "fundamentals" I mean principles such as

- find defects early
- understand your requirements before you design
- test before you release
- plan and define your process before you implement
- and so on...

However, I don't believe what I recommend is actually opposite to these principles at all. It just seems that way because what many of us were thinking when the fundamentals were first explained to us has turned out to be quite different from what actually works.

I would also like to point out that I am not the first person to have observed this phenomenon, and it is not unique to software development. As the immortal Yogi Berra once said, *"In theory there is no difference between theory and practice. In practice there is."*[1]

I don't believe this situation implies there is necessarily anything inherently wrong with many long held software

---

[1]http://c2.com/cgi/wiki?DifferenceBetweenTheoryAndPractice

engineering fundamentals. But there is a very real problem centering on common misbeliefs related to **how to** best achieve many of our well established software engineering guiding principles. These misbeliefs are tied to the **activities people think they need to conduct**, "**how much**" of those activities they need to conduct, and "**when**" they need to conduct them, to effectively implement software engineering fundamentals.

What is in this book

In this book I provide true software development stories that may challenge long held thinking. I highlight **26 upside down principles** along with upside down principle **clarifying thoughts**. At the end of each story you will find **extended clarifying thoughts** in the upside down principle summary sections. I also highlight 18 coaching tips that can help you get your organization "right side up" with respect to performance.

If you are wondering if a book that highlights coaching tips is for you, it is. I believe everyone in an organization should view themselves as a coach. In order to help coaches everywhere, in Part II of the book I have framed the highlighted principles and coaching tips that have materialized from my stories within a framework I like to use called Essence. I find Essence to be a remarkably straightforward medium for communicating software development practices and fostering collaboration, even among non-technical stakeholders.

If you have not heard of Essence yet, you have probably heard of the foundation from which it evolved, which I explain further in Part II. I will explain more below how Essence relates to my stories and coaching tips. If you choose to read

Part II, I think you will agree that Essence is quite useful for capturing and describing these lessons, tips and best practices, and I hope you will be able to find ways to make Essence useful in your own work.

About Essence

In the stories in this book you will learn many questions that I asked my clients and coaching tips I gave them to help them overcome common obstacles and achieve higher performance. Many of the questions I ask and the tips I provide are based on experience. But what if there was a way to share these questions and tips with practitioners in a form they could easily access when a coach isn't immediately available?

I have been involved since 2010 in the development of a new framework, referred to as Essence [1, 2, 3, 4], that provides a way to do just that. I sometimes refer to Essence as a "thinking framework," but, in fact, Essence is more than just a "thinking framework". Essence provides a "common ground" set of essentials relevant to all software development efforts. This includes a set of checklists that can stimulate the kinds of questions that I ask my clients. You will learn more about these questions in my stories in Part I of this book.

Essence also includes a way for anyone, including consultants, coaches, practice/method authors and practitioners, to express their practices and tips in a common language highlighting the unique discriminators of their approach. This way of expressing practices in the Essence language is referred to as "essentialization."

In Part II of this book I provide an introduction to Essence, and a simple example of an "essentialized" practice that is similar to a practice I created for one of my clients discussed in Part I of this book. I also provide in Part II a summary of the 26 upside down principles in an essentialized form. You will also learn in Part II how anyone can use the Essence language to capture the questions that should be asked– in a checklist form– and the activities recommended to be conducted, such as those I share in Part I of this book.

How to use this book

I highly recommend that you read all the stories in this book straight through from beginning to end. As one of my reviewers commented, the book is short enough to be read in 3 hours. Then, use Part II to review the principles and learn about the Essence framework including the checklists related to each story. A cross-reference is provided in Part II from each essentialized principle back to the relevant story in Part I.

Another way to use this book, for those who don't have time to read all the stories, is to jump directly to Part II where you can learn about Essence, review the principles and related checklists, and then jump back and read just the stories you are most interested in.

Why I wrote this book

This is not a book about theory. The stories I share are all true. I wrote this book because I believe the stories, together with the principles, principle clarifying thoughts, coaching tips and related Essence framework checklists can stimulate deeper reflection and discussion helping you discover your own best "how to" software engineering approaches within your organization.

About the stories in this book

The stories in this book demonstrate what I have learned about how predictable performance is achieved in organizations today. In the past we have spent significant effort training our people by focusing on "defined processes"[2] and "best practices"[2]. But true stories of what has been proven to work are better at communicating **"how much"** of certain activities need to be conducted, **"when"** those activities should be conducted, and **"exactly what activities should be conducted,"** which is what most practitioners want to know.

Sharing stories works because when people hear true stories about how another team handled a problem similar to their own they can often quickly translate that experience to their own situation. "Defined processes" and "best practices", on the other hand–specifically the way they have often been communicated in the past– leave too many important questions unanswered. Once you understand this fact, it can lead you to think differently about many of our long held fundamental principles. Let me give you an example.

---

[2]Some organizations use the term "process" and others use the term "practice" to mean the written description of how they would like their people to behave. But the practices (or processes) that people actually follow may not be written down (i.e. they are tacit). In this book I use the term "practice" and "process" interchangeably and I mean it to include both types—written and tacit.

Do we really need to define our processes?

A fundamental many of us were taught is that we need to define our processes and train our people in our processes prior to using the processes on a real project. We have also been taught the importance of ensuring our teams are using our defined processes in a consistent repeatable way before trying to improve them [5]. In other words, many of us have believed for years that we need to focus on defining, training and achieving repeatable basic processes within our teams before we focus on raising the performance of our team.

Now, I understand why this fundamental notion seems to make sense in theory. But let me tell you a little bit about what I now do with most of my clients that seems upside down from this fundamental principle– but has proven to work.

First, I spend very little time defining a process before I ask my client to try it out by using it, and I often encourage them to use it on a real project, rather than in a pilot environment. This is clearly not what I was taught to do. Now don't misunderstand me. I am not saying you shouldn't define your processes and train your people before asking them to use the processes. Nor am I suggesting you should try out completely unproven ideas on critical projects before you have any idea at all if they might work. You will learn more in Story Two of this book why I have found this approach works best in practice.

But now let me share a related idea to help you understand some of my thinking. What I have learned is that most companies today that are doing software development and know they have weaknesses and want to improve already have a way of working that has strengths as well as weaknesses. It may not be a repeatable institutionalized process that is used consistently across the entire organization. But there almost always exists, even in organizations that operate almost entirely in an ad hoc manner, at least one project, or group of people on a project, that have established their own way of working that is working well and proving successful. This has been my experience.

When organizations begin asking questions about improving their way of working, or even considering trying something completely new, it is usually because they know they can do better. And many of them know they can do better because part of their organization actually is doing better and they are ready to start using those proven best practices right now so they can perform better too.

Once organizations arrive at this point, what I have found to be most effective to help them move forward is twofold. First, they need some simple guidance and coaching in how to capture what is already working well– even if it is only for a small group in their organization– and spread it to others in their organization. Second, they need help identifying where their most critical weaknesses lie that are hurting their performance, and they need help figuring out the most important changes they can make right now to their current way of working to address these clear weaknesses. It is often in this area where critical weaknesses exist that the best opportunities to try something new are found.

Upside Down Principle One:

 Traditional thinking: Plan and define your process before you use your process.

 Clarifying thought: Conduct just enough planning for your team to get started moving forward.

More reasons not to spend a lot of effort defining processes before using them

I have also found that it can become a wasteful exercise to spend more than a minimum amount of effort documenting processes that have not already been proven to work successfully in your specific organization. For this reason, I have moved away from putting much effort into process definition up front. The best time to put significant effort into documenting processes is after–not before– we know what works. On real projects every day teams learn and every day those teams should feel empowered and encouraged to improve the way they work based on what they are learning on the job. Unfortunately, what happens too often is that organizations spend far **too much effort** trying to define their processes in detail before their teams actually use and prove out those processes on real endeavors.

This strategy inevitably leads to internal organizational struggles between those who are being asked to use the processes (e.g. the practitioners on the job who are trying to develop quality software for their customers) and those who defined the processes based on what has come to be referred to as "industry best practices." Let me give you another example.

Are industry "best practices" best for you?

Now, once again, don't misunderstand me. I have nothing against industry best practices. In fact, a large part of what I do with my clients is sharing industry best practices trying to enlighten them when I see weaknesses in their current way of working where what other organizations have learned could help. But the problem is, while many common misapplications of fundamentals repeat in the software industry, the answer can never be found completely in any single "best practice" solution proven somewhere else in a different organization than your own. This is not to say you can't learn from the experiences of others. But it is to say your situation will always have your own **unique conditions and constraints** that your organization needs to think about as you consider lessons and best practices from other organizations and industry in general.

Stated another way, while industry best practices and lessons are great, they do not alleviate each organization from listening to their practitioners, understanding their needs and understanding the specific needs and constraints of their stakeholders, environment and their product.

 **Upside Down Principle Two:**

 <u>Traditional thinking</u>: Focus your improvement efforts on industry "best practices".

 <u>Clarifying thought</u>: Focus your improvement effort on your team, stakeholders and environment.

Is process or performance more important to you?

We have for a long time been hearing about the importance of defining your process first, sharing industry best practices, and sharing lessons learned as keys to improvement. While I do not dispute the value in these proven approaches to improve performance, the way they have been implemented in the past has led many organizational improvement efforts to fall far short of their goals. It is my belief, based on my 40 plus years of working in this industry, at least part of the reason that the software engineering community continues to face this problem is because the emphasis on how to go about improving performance has been significantly misplaced.

Performance itself should be the primary focus. Process is secondary. Unfortunately, the tail has been wagging the dog far too long and this is at least part of the reason why I titled this book: *It's All Upside Down.*

Summary Upside Down Principles 1, 2

<u>Principle One</u>: *Plan and define your process before you use your process*

<u>Extended clarifying thought</u>: Conduct just enough planning and definition for your team to move forward using the key processes needed to get started so they can prove them out, and refine them with improvements that work best for their situation.

Note: This is an example of what I meant when I referred to the need to communicate "when" certain activities and "how much" of those activities need to be conducted.

<u>Principle Two</u>: *Focus your improvement efforts on industry "best practices"*

<u>Extended clarifying thought</u>: While industry best practices and lessons are useful, they cannot replace listening to your practitioners, understanding their needs and understanding the specific needs and constraints of your stakeholders, environment and your product.

PART I

Story One: Do You Really Need Measures to Improve?

A fundamental principle many of us were taught is that we need measures to improve. We've all heard statements such as:

"You can't manage, if you don't measure" and

"If you can't measure what you are doing, you don't know what you are doing" and

"Without measures you will never know for sure if you really improved"

These statements on face value seem hard to argue with. So many organizations that are trying to improve performance spend significant effort putting a measurement program in place before they think seriously about improving the way they work.

A measurement program can be a good and useful thing if it's set up in a way that works for the organization. But before we talk about that, let's step back and ask the question: Do we necessarily need a measurement program to address a problem that is obvious to the organization?

Should you really set up a measurement program right now?

Now, please understand my point. To set up a measurement

program the right way takes considerable effort up front. First, you need to look at your own business and, specifically, your business objectives. You need to ask:

"What are our goals?"

Then you need to ask:

"How will we know if we are on track to achieving our goals?"

Then you need to ask:

"What can we measure to help us in this assessment?"

When organizations start down this path often it requires multiple brainstorming sessions and discussions about measures which frequently end up flowing down into the organization where derived measures need to be gathered, aggregated, and analyzed periodically. Often this effort takes significant resources away from direct project activities that create revenue for the organization.

So let's now step back. I am not here intending to argue with the value of setting up a measurement program. If you are considering setting up a measurement program in your organization that might be a great thing to do. But I just want you to think a bit about where your organization is, and if that is the best area to expend energy right now given where your organization is. Now I want to give you a simple example to help you as you think about this.

Does your organization suffer from the common problem of constant "interrupts"?

A common problem I often see in client organizations is the software team constantly dealing with interrupts due to the latest crisis in the organization. Constant interruptions can create significant disruption degrading any chance for the team maintaining a predictable velocity. This particularly affects organizations that are trying to implement agile/Scrum practices, which require the team to plan and commit to a fixed iteration length and an agreed to set of backlog items to complete.

One approach that I have seen used in an organization to try to address this problem is for the team to start measuring interrupts. I will refer to this organization as NANO. The thinking is that if we can gather real data that shows management the impact of the interrupts, then management might understand why it is so important that we do something to change the interrupt driven culture.

On the surface this sounds like a great approach, and I have heard many people agree that the idea is a good one. I have also observed multiple organizations take this approach to help bring to light this important issue they would like to solve. I have even seen one organization go so far as to have software team personnel enter a ticket in their ticket system that allows them to identify each interrupt, how many hours they spent on the interrupt, and a brief description of the interrupt.

This data allowed the interrupts to be analyzed and grouped into categories. Then a graph showing the cost of various categories of interrupts could be created and shared with management or any other personnel who might be able to take action to potentially help change the interrupt-driven culture of the organization.

Now, understand that I think this is a great idea. Measuring team interrupts could even be a derived measure in a measurement system where one of the organizational agreed to business objectives is to achieve predictable product releases.

Such a measure could potentially help contribute to achieving this goal by bringing to light a problem that is hurting the organization's performance, related to achieving predictable releases. An organization could even decide to use the interrupt measures gathered to predict future performance by building into their plan anticipated interrupts based on past interrupt frequency. But this leads to an important question:

Is measuring interrupts the best approach to solve the common interrupt problem we see in many organizations?

A different approach to solve the common problem of "interrupts"

Let me now share another approach that I observed a different organization take that allowed them to solve their interrupt problem in a surprisingly short period of time without first measuring the frequency and impact of their interrupts. This organization I will refer to as NORO. NORO had a culture of always reacting to the latest fire-drill by throwing everyone on the problem as soon as it occurred. Interrupts could come to the software team from various sources and at any time. The accepted culture in the organization was for the team to drop everything and immediately solve the problem especially when the interrupt came from the VP of Operations, or from one of their key customer support people.

I was hired by NORO because they knew they needed to put some process discipline in place, and the recognition of this need started at the top of the company with the president who hired me. When I began to understand how this organization was operating, it quickly became clear to me that we needed to start with basic management practices. I conducted basic Scrum training for the software team. During this training I facilitated a risk brainstorming session to get out on the table any concerns people had that could derail the use of the new Scrum practices.

During this brainstorming session, the Scrum Master, whom I was training, said that the biggest risk he saw was that we were only training the software team. He expressed concern that the rest of the organization would continue to work the same way they had always worked. He was concerned that the software team would never be able to succeed in their planned sprints, if the interrupts continued.

Strangely, once we began the sprints the interrupts seemed to vanish. At the first sprint retrospective we discussed why we seemed to have solved the big risk of interrupts. The Scrum Master reasoned he wasn't getting interrupts because most of his interrupts came from a key customer service representative who had been tapped to become the product owner. Because that customer service representative under-stood his new role as product owner, and his responsibilities with regard to all work going on the product backlog and being prioritized before worked on, he understood the new way of working and had stopped with his interrupt behavior.

The president of the company had also taken it upon himself to learn the new process and had attended the Scrum training. He also participated in the first sprint retrospective. During that retrospective he said that the reason the VP of Opera-tions wasn't interrupting anymore was because he had been keeping the VP up to speed on the new way of working and what the team was working on.

What everyone realized was that we solved the interrupt problem by solving the real reason people interrupted. We put a new way of working in place, and we refined it on a real project. Because the effort was supported by the president and key influential stakeholders, the employees understood that the company was serious about operating differently and so the new behavior just happened. We didn't need to measure the cost of interrupts first to prove what everyone knew was hurting performance. Everyone knew the interrupts were hurting performance so they just all agreed to change their behavior.

Upside Down Principle Three:

 Traditional thinking: You need to establish measures first to be sure any process changes lead to real performance improvement.

 Clarifying thought: Sometimes it's easier to just fix a problem than worrying about how to measure the effectiveness of your solution.

What happened in the organization that measured their interrupts?

In the NANO organization where they measured the cost of interrupts some interesting things happened. When we analyzed the interrupt data we found that many of the entries people had logged as interrupts didn't sound like activities that should have been treated as interrupts. Many of them were normal activities that could have been predicted and planned for, if the team had done a more thorough job of thinking ahead of time about all of the work that would need to be done in the upcoming sprint. I am going to give you an example below.

The first lesson learned was that the team had been taking too narrow a view of the scope of work to be done in the upcoming sprint by just looking at the items on the product backlog, rather than including all work that was likely to be needed to be done. This effort also uncovered the fact that many roles in the organization needed to be reviewed from the standpoint of responsibilities. This occurred because what some people were calling interrupts should have been viewed as a normal part of their job responsibilities.

For example, a technical lead who was also a developer was viewing requests to review a developer's work as an interrupt. So the interesting thing we learned by measuring interrupts at NANO was that there weren't really as many interrupts going on as many people thought. People needed refresher training in their own responsibilities and how to estimate their capacity and effort required to complete certain tasks, given those responsibilities. You will hear more about how we helped NANO with their interrupt problem later in this book.

Clearly, if you can figure out the root of the problem and just solve it as we saw in the second case, it is the ideal approach. But in many organizations this isn't as easy as it was at NORO. In many organizations where I have seen interrupt data measured and shared with management, too often no action results to change the interrupt behavior.

What else should you do, if you decide to measure interrupts?

In some cases measuring may be the best you can do, but if you take this approach I suggest you capture some information about what the interrupt is and how much time the interrupt is costing you. Then you should analyze the interrupts and see if you can categorize them into certain types ("or buckets") of interrupts. This might lead you to develop a graph where you can see which categories are costing the organization the most.

Don't be surprised if you find yourself refining your categories as you conduct this analysis. But my suggestion is don't stop with just analyzing the data. You should go further. I suggest you talk to people in your organization, and hold some brainstorming sessions to come up with possible approaches to solve the interrupts—especially the most costly ones– before you take the results of your analysis to management.

You might even suggest that people try some of the ideas you come up with on real projects. Showing management data that can be used to explain what is going on in the organization is good, but bringing a proposed solution is better. And it is even better yet, if you can point to a real project that is using your proposed solution as evidence that it works.

Upside Down Principle Four:

 Traditional thinking: Showing management hard data related to a problem is the best way to get them to support a needed process change.

Clarifying thought: Showing management a proven solution is better than showing them hard data about a problem.

Why the interrupts vanished at NORO

In NOROs case the interrupts went away without measuring them because they implemented a way of working that eliminated the root cause of the interrupts. Note here that I use the phrase "way of working" rather than "process". This is intentional because for many people the word "process" implies a "documented process" that has been reviewed, approved, placed under control, and trained in a formal manner.

Rather, when I say "way of working" I am talking about a set of activities that people use because they recognize how those activities can achieve a desired result. In the NANO organization we learned that the interrupt problem could be substantially reduced through on-the-job coaching of responsibilities associated with certain team roles and coaching related to effective sprint planning. In the NORO case when someone came with a potential interrupt, it wasn't *"drop everything and solve it immediately"* anymore. It was

"Go see Jim, and he will place it on the backlog."

Soon everyone at NORO understood that this was the new way of working. Because people understood the new behavior with the new way of working, the interrupts just stopped happening.

Summary Upside Down Principles 3, 4

<u>Principle Three:</u> *You need to establish measures first to be sure any process changes lead to real performance improvement*

<u>Extended clarifying thought:</u> In general measuring is important to be sure you aren't fooling yourself, but sometimes it's easier to just fix the problem when everyone agrees and you know how to fix it.

<u>Principle Four:</u> *Showing management hard data related to a problem is the best way to get them to support a needed process change*

<u>Extended clarifying thought:</u> Showing management hard data related to a problem, along with hard data that demonstrates a real solution that has been proven to work is the best way to get them to support a needed process change. Often, in cases where the problem relates to interrupts, solutions to root causes are found in helping team members understand the full extent of their responsibilities.

Story Two: Do You Want a Repeatable Process or Repeatable Results?

Anyone who has taken courses on process improvement or read much about process improvement frameworks knows about the importance of having a defined repeatable process to effectively manage a software effort.

But do we really need repeatable processes to achieve repeatable results?

The common argument often heard goes something like this:

"If you don't use a defined repeatable process then you can't be confident in predicting how long your effort will take, and you can't be sure you will have a high quality bug-free product when done."

While on the surface this sounds reasonable, in practice there are some interesting things that often happen with software teams that could lead you to rethink what type of processes you really need for project success. Furthermore, surveys conducted at Ambysoft [6] by Scott Ambler indicate that people want repeatable results over repeatable processes.

Background on two clients

In the next few stories I am going to share with you more

about two of my clients that took different paths to improve their software performance. I will also continue to use these two organizations throughout the remainder of the book to illustrate other stories. Both had common goals of reducing latent defects and improving their track record at getting high quality software products delivered to their customers while meeting schedule commitments.

The two clients I will discuss you have already heard a little bit about in the previous story– NORO and NANO. But let me tell you a little more about both of them now. Both NORO and NANO had a history of too many latent defects finding their way into released software products resulting in dissatisfied customers. NANO had well-defined CMMI [5] level 3 processes that their software teams used and had a good track record of meeting their schedule commitments for customer deliveries. But many of these deliveries had latent defects that often caused a major crisis in the organization when discovered after delivery. When a typical crisis occurred it would often lead to unanticipated interrupts in subsequent planned work in order to get patch releases delivered to fix the customer-reported "critical" problems.

As bad as this situation was at NANO, NORO had a worse track record in that they not only had frequent customer reported problems after delivery that caused constant interrupts back to their software teams, but NORO couldn't even get their releases out on time. Part of the problem at NORO was the fact that NORO didn't have processes even close to CMMI level 2. NORO ran most of their projects in an ad hoc fashion with no defined processes. This was the situation at NORO when they first engaged me to help them.

Now let me tell you a little more about NORO. NORO is a new

client of mine that I started working with late in 2015. When they contracted me they were very open about their situation as having no defined processes, and they recognized– especially due to the growth they were currently experiencing– that they needed to add some process discipline.

Typical approach when using the CMMI

Typically, when I am working with an organization that wants to improve their performance using the CMMI framework we start by discussing how they operate today and we look to find gaps in their processes that are hurting their performance. To be honest, if the organization is seeking to conduct a formal CMMI appraisal to achieve a specific CMMI maturity level on a specified timeline, this often leads us to place emphasis in areas that may not be the most critical to the organization's performance.

As an example, when I first started working with NORO, even though they had no documented processes I quickly determined the criticality of risk management given the problems they were facing with key customers. Risk Management is a CMMI maturity level 3 process area, and therefore, if NORO had been seeking a CMMI maturity level 2 appraisal with a critical deadline to achieving it, I probably would not have put the high focus on the risk management area as I did early with NORO.

However, because NORO was not seeking a specific CMMI maturity level on a critical scheduled deadline, I was able to focus my coaching efforts on the real pain points that were holding back this organization from achieving their schedule commitments and delivering high quality bug-free products.

I started at NORO by coaching their development team in five basic Scrum practices (Backlog Development and Refinement,

Sprint Planning, Daily Standups, Sprint Review and Sprint Retrospective). These practices actually go a long way toward helping any organization achieve CMMI maturity level 2 because they address many of the expected practices within the Project Planning, Project Monitor and Control, Measurement and Analysis, and Requirement Management process areas within the CMMI framework.

Nevertheless, the real pain points that were seriously hurting NORO related to risks that they had with changes they would make to their product to address issues raised by one client, while these same changes would produce unintended consequences breaking functionality that was critical to another client.

They also had to deal with the constant risk of problem reports being submitted at any time from one client who demanded a fix within 24 hours. This requirement to fix reported problems within a 24 hour window was actually in their contract with one key client. This situation had led the company to become a reactive, drop everything, and address today's crisis kind of company.

One of my first high priority observations that needed to be addressed at NORO was the pain the teams were experiencing due to their poor risk management approach. On further analysis I also realized this pain point tied closely to their poor approach to testing and peer reviews.

From a CMMI perspective—without thinking about what it would take to achieve a specific maturity level— the process areas I was most worried about given what I was observing were Risk Management, Verification, and Validation. But this was counter to what I had been taught as to where to start when you see an organization with no defined processes and running in an ad hoc fashion. Risk Management, Verification and Validation are all CMMI maturity level 3 process areas within the CMMI framework.

This leads to a question:

If an organization is using the CMMI framework, how much emphasis should you place on the CMMI Process Area levels when guiding the organization with a performance improvement strategy?

The right approach when using the CMMI framework

Now, to be honest, if you talk to people who have been involved with the development of the CMMI model and understand the model's intent, many of them will tell you that the approach I take with clients by focusing first on the real pain that is clearly hurting the organization's performance is exactly the right strategy to take. They will tell you that the CMMI framework is a model, and that:

"All models are wrong, but some are useful."

[7]

Upside Down Principle Five:

 Traditional thinking: If you use the CMMI framework you need to focus on the level 2 process areas before attacking level 3 (refer to staged implementation of CMMI).

Clarifying thought: The CMMI is a guide, not a set of dictated ordered processes.

Reflection on the CMMI

But isn't this upside down from what the CMMI framework tells us we should do?

Actually no, if you use the model as intended. The point is that we should not be a slave to the CMMI process area levels in determining the best strategy to improve a given organization's performance. If it makes sense to tackle issues at a higher CMMI maturity level because of certain **specific conditions**, then go ahead and do it. This is an example where effective coaches and process improvement professionals can guide organizations in making the best decisions for their specific organization given their specific situation.

It is unfortunate that this common sense approach to performance improvement has gotten drowned out by many consultants/lead appraisers who have become blinded by the CMMI model structure and the pressures they allow themselves to give in to when assessing and guiding an organization that is driving to achieve a specific CMMI maturity level by a specific date.

Why recommendations sound upside down, but aren't

To help explain why some of my recommendations may sound upside down, but aren't, let me now go back and explain what we did at NORO where I didn't have to deal with the conflicting pressures of a schedule that said we need to achieve a CMMI level X by date ABC.

In the past my first reaction would have been—regardless of whether my client was trying to achieve a specific CMMI level or not – to start by guiding them in developing a well-defined set of processes on how NORO should work, and then run a pilot project to prove out these processes. Then, after the pilot project, roll out the processes to others in the organization through formal classroom training.

This sounds like the right thing to do and is consistent with what has been taught for years related to process improvement and best practices. But now let me share with you a little more background information on NORO and what we did at NORO that convinced me this approach is upside down.

Why NORO got rid of their heavy-weight processes

NORO is a small organization (less than 100 people) with a Department of Defense (DoD) contractor heritage that began with an agile-vision in order to respond rapidly to changing customer needs. This vision was in part a reaction of the founders who sought to escape the bureaucratic-slow-moving world of their previous organization's heavyweight CMMI-based processes. However, in 2015 as NORO experienced growth they realized they had gone too far in dropping traditional processes and needed to add back a level of process discipline. In October 2015 I was engaged by NORO to help them in their improvement journey. [3] [8]

How we got things moving at NORO

In the improvement effort kickoff meeting at NORO we discussed pain points, success criteria, organizational culture, policies, and constraints. During initial discussions it became clear that fundamental work management practices were a priority.

To get the effort moving I gave the team a two-hour training session including five basic Scrum practices. [9]

---

[3] Parts of the NORO story have been extracted from previously published material found in the article title, "CMMI the Agile Way in Constrained and Regulated Environments", Crosstalk, Journal of Defense Software, July/August 2016.

The agreed approach was one where the team would learn by using the new practices, as described in the training, on a real project. I coached them through the sprints by taking on the role of their Scrum Master while also training an internal Scrum Master and Product Owner.

The agreed approach included a planned release to actual customers at the conclusion of the third sprint. In other words, we were not just piloting these new processes. They were being used for real on an actual project as the team learned the new way of working driving for a formal released product to key customers. The initial documentation that the team had on how to execute the five Scrum practices was only my training slides (34 slides) and the official Scrum guide. [9]

Why I spend little time documenting

Note: The four examples described below are examples of what I meant in the introduction to this book when I referred to **"exactly what activities should be conducted".**

One of the reasons I don't like to spend much time documenting processes early on an improvement effort is because I have never seen two organizations implement Scrum (or for that matter, any defined process) the same way. And even when an organization tries to roll out a common repeatable organizational "agile/Scrum" process, as soon as the individual teams start to implement retrospective improvements they immediately begin to diverge. This is not a bad thing, especially because the areas in which they diverge are usually based on their own experiences related to how to best accomplish a key performance goal in their specific situation. Let me give you some examples. [8]

Ex. 1: Why teams vary in their activities to achieve key performance goals

NORO has many customers that use their core product. To address varying customer needs the product is configurable. A common problem NORO faces is changes made to address one customer's reported defects, too often cause unintended negative consequences in the way another customer uses the product.

In NORO's case, discussions around this problem led to actions accepted by the product owner to conduct meetings with two critical stakeholders most likely to be in disagreement based on past product releases. The agreed goal was to get key representatives from each stakeholder organization to attend an internal sprint review to gain early feedback before the next formal release of the product. This discussion uncovered the fact that one critical stakeholder would not be able to attend the sprint review due to a conflict. Therefore a plan was put in place to deliver the early product version on site to this customer to pro-actively gain their early feedback prior to formal release. Note how the plan that we put in place was based on **project specific conditions**. Given different project conditions, the right solution could and should vary.

Ex. 2: Why teams vary in their activities to achieve key performance goals

As another example, when I was contracted to help NORO they were very open in telling me they knew they needed help with their testing approach. They did not have formal written test procedures, although they did have an independent test group, and they did have an independent quality control department that was required to approve each product release before shipment to any customer.

Initially we planned to defer improving test practices at NORO until a later sprint because we did not want to take on too much change in the organization all at once which could cause our improvement effort to fail. However, because the reactionary interrupt-driven culture was causing serious pain in the organization, I recommended that we raise the priority and start putting some small test improvements in place immediately on the very first sprint. In many organizations I would not have recommended this. I had to weigh the benefits against the risks, and in this case the benefits of getting test improvements moving immediately outweighed the risks.

The first improvement to address this pain point was to initiate a three-sprint cycle where every third sprint would be a formal release. Previously NORO did not have a well-defined product release process. This release process didn't require all customers to necessarily install the new release every third sprint, but it did require the NORO team to work to that possibility. With the three-sprint cycle we instituted a plan where in the third sprint of each cycle only 50% capacity of developers would be used for new functionality, and the other 50% would be used for increased testing– focusing specifically on regression testing in preparation for the release.

Previous to this recommendation NORO had no regression test suite. Some of NORO's customer support representatives expressed concern that with the new frequent release approach that certain customers might misunderstand the expected capabilities in each release. To address this potential risk the product owner accepted the responsibility to directly contact key customers prior to each release informing them ahead of time exactly what functionality was planned for each new release and what features would be coming in future releases.

Upside Down Principle Six:

 Traditional thinking: You should have a well-defined repeatable test process, and always test completely with a goal of zero defects before you release.

Clarifying thought: Some defects are acceptable to your customer—be open and honest about them.

Ex. 3 Why teams vary in their activities to achieve key performance goals

During the first sprint at NORO in a daily standup one of the developers said that, "bugs often come back". This led to a discussion and the team agreed that they should capture the tests they run to fix bugs and run these tests again in an automated way. Previously they had been continually re-inventing their tests every sprint and running them manually.

One of the developers agreed to develop a test code template that everyone could use to build their automated unit tests. As it turned out automating their unit tests was not as easy as the team first thought, but they didn't abandon the idea. They discussed at their retrospective the difficulties they encountered and then agreed to some changes in their approach for the next sprint.

***Ex. 4 Why teams vary in their activities to achieve key
performance goals***

As another example, one of the testers complained during a
retrospective that when the developers were completing tasks
they were not providing clear direction to the testers on how
to test the change. The developers agreed that they could do
better, and accepted the action to provide clearer notes to the
testers.

In a subsequent retrospective we heard that same tester say
that the testing direction had improved. I asked the developers
what they were doing differently that had helped the communication with the testers. One developer replied:

*"I am thinking much more about the notes I place in the ticket
to explain to the tester what it is he needs to do. I start the note
out to the tester with: 'This is what you need to do...'"*

I asked him if this means he explains how to set up for the test
as well as exactly what to look for? He replied,

*"Yes, exactly. I am making it much more clear what he needs
to do to test my change."*

I also asked:

*"Are you also thinking about possible unintended conse-
quences? For example, areas you might have broken, but you
didn't have time to test?"*

He replied,

"We can do better in that area."

And the developers all agreed to accept the action to make
improvements in capturing notes for the testers related to
potential breakage areas, and they would work this improvement in the next sprint.

Reflection on how NORO improved performance

We started NORO on the path to improvement in their very first sprint with a small improvement related to a developer's suggestion along with multiple other improvements related to stakeholder communication, release process and regression testing. These improvements continued over the first six sprints which led to not only improved low level testing, but improved integration testing and regression testing. Each sprint the team made testing improvements based on what they had learned in the previous sprint and based on the goal of significantly reducing defects that escaped to the customer.

You have heard multiple examples how NORO began to continuously improve their practices in small steps. As the team improved, I kept notes that I eventually captured as hints and additional checklists as part of the formal process documentation.

Upside Down Principle Seven:

 Traditional thinking: You have to prove out your processes on a pilot project before using them for real.

Clarifying thought: Prove out your process on a project that reflects the real conditions your practitioners most often face.

What I want to emphasize is that neither I, nor anyone else, could have possibly written a process as useful as the one we eventually wrote after running a number of real sprints on a real project that included real product releases to customers. The process we eventually documented was one that had been proven to work, not on a lab-like theoretical "pilot" project. But proven on a project that reflected the real challenges that NORO team members face each day.

Some might argue that the approach we took at NORO is too risky by asking:

"How can you allow your team to– in effect– discover their best practices while actually working on a real customer project?"

Some might also argue that what we did was upside down with respect to the fundamental principle of defining your process first and proving your process before rolling it out to a real project team. While I understand the rationale behind this argument, I counter this position with real experiences that I have seen work. The fact is you can't create the best practices in a lab-like environment. You can only create them in an environment that matches the real challenges your team will face.

Upside Down Principle Eight:

Traditional thinking:You need to hold your processes stable during a project to avoid risk.

Clarifying thought: The real goal is repeatable results, not a repeatable controlled stable process.

I also counter arguments against the NORO approach in that there is actually more risk in forcing an unproven process on a team and holding it constant under the premise of the need to maintain a stable process. This is because, in fact, until the process is proven in a real project environment it is likely that it is not the best process to be using. And forcing the wrong process on a team is likely to hinder rather than help progress.

Evidence of measurable improvement

Surveys conducted with NORO leadership, development team members and NORO stakeholders confirmed measurable improved performance through reduced defects escaping to the customer. These survey results were validated with quantifiable data indicating a 100% improvement in team productivity.

I want to highlight how improvements began to happen at NORO. Most practical and useful improvements start out small and continue incrementally and are discovered and implemented by the team. The improved way of working at NORO related to testing practices was eventually captured and documented so that when new developers came into the organization they could quickly get up to speed on the agreed testing approach at NORO.

Why waiting to document isn't "upside down"

As NORO was moving into their fourth sprint I was reducing my involvement in their day to day project activities. I then created "lite" documentation for 9 practices that NORO was using. Each practice was documented using a 3 page template that included a brief description of the purpose of the practice, activities to conduct, products to work with, roles required, when the practice was typically conducted, and a set of 3 checklists that provided reminders to the team for things to consider when preparing to conduct the practice, things to consider during the practice, and things to consider before completion of the practice.

An important point that I want to highlight here is that the checklists were developed directly from what the team had learned when conducting the practices during the actual project sprint activities, including improvements that the team members themselves came up with during their retrospective discussions.

It is worth noting here that this is where agile and CMMI come together. Agile isn't opposed to documentation, it just wants to prevent documentation as waste. This approach ensures that by the time we are documenting the process, it has already proven valuable and now the documentation of the process in turn becomes valuable for educating current and future team members on this established approach.

It is also worth noting that Essence checklists were used to help the team get started, but the checklists we added were **specific to what the team had learned**.

Essence checklists are good to help teams get a conversation going about the right things the team needs to be talking about to get better. However, we found in many cases more specific checklists were needed to help the NORO team continue to keep improving their performance. See example below.

It is also important to note that I could not have produced these checklists at the start of the project because many of the checklists reflected what the team had learned through each sprint. As an example, in NORO's unit test practice the checklist items for things to think about "before completion" included:

· *Ensure test cases are clear for the tester. Before completing a coding ticket, each developer should think about the tests that the tester should run to verify this change. The test should not be just a repeat of the developer's unit tests, but a test that is conducted more from the user perspective.*

· *Recommend appropriate regression tests. Before completing the coding ticket, developers should think about possible impacts to other areas, and make appropriate suggestions for regression testing to the tester.*

· *If the change is isolated with little likelihood of impact, place a note in the ticket letting the tester know that minimal regression testing is needed.*

While one could argue that these checklists could be *"best practice"* reminders for software developers in any software organization, these checklists specifically were added as a result of retrospective discussions at NORO where the team realized the value of each of these reminders in helping them reduce the likelihood of latent defects. When a team understands why a checklist item exists, they are more likely to take the checklist item seriously and use it as NORO did leading to real performance improvement.

Upside Down Principle Nine:

 Traditional thinking:You have to produce your process documentation before your teams use your processes on real projects.

Clarifying thought: The most useful documentation reflects what the team has learned from performing the process.

Summary Upside Down Principles 5, 6, 7, 8, 9

<u>Principle Five</u>: *If you use the CMMI framework you need to focus on the level 2 process areas before attacking level 3*

<u>Extended clarifying thought</u>: The CMMI framework is a model. No model reflects real situations perfectly. Use it as a guide, not a set of dictated, ordered processes.

<u>Principle Six</u>: *You should have a well-defined repeatable test process, and always test completely with a goal of zero defects before you release*

<u>Extended clarifying thought</u>: Often in today's fast-paced competitive world organizations don't have enough time to test everything completely before each release. One practical and proven approach is to test just the pieces your team has focused on during this release, and any prior released functionality to ensure it still works. Then aggressively focus on letting everyone know the limitations of what is in the current release. This means being open and honest with what this release does and does not do, and what will be coming in future releases.

<u>Principle Seven</u>: *You have to prove out your processes on a pilot project before using them for real*

<u>Extended clarifying thought</u>: Experience has shown that the best place to prove out your processes is on a real project that exhibits the same kind of challenges teams typically face each day.

<u>Principle Eight</u>: *You need to hold your processes stable during a project to avoid risk*

Extended clarifying thought: Allowing your team to "continually tune their use of the practices and tools" as they learn, and doing so in small steps that can be reviewed and revised as necessary in short iterations– while it may seem upside down from what we have been taught– is actually the best way to achieve real and sustainable repeatable results. And the real goal is repeatable results, not a repeatable controlled stable process.

It is also worth emphasizing here that such tuning needs to be done within a structure that provides clear limits to acceptable tuning. Otherwise we risk chaos.

Principle Nine: *You have to produce your process documentation before your teams use your processes on real projects*

Extended clarifying thought: Teams do need to know how to use key practices and tools selected for your project. But key practices and tools often provide just a starting point for what practitioners need to know to perform well on most projects. As an example, they need checklists with reminders, and you can't produce the most useful checklists at the start of the project because many of the most useful checklists reflect what the team learns while performing on a real project.

Story Three: Upside Down Path to Fewer Defects

In this story I discuss six categories of "escaping defects" found in one of my client organizations, along with how I helped the team improve their performance by reducing future occurrences of these types of defects. What I hope the reader learns from this story is how traditional thinking on many causes of common escaping defects often misses the mark when it comes to helping practitioners improve performance.

During the first week of February, 2016 as I wrote NORO's process documentation I received an email and some data from the quality manager at NANO. A few months earlier we had initiated a performance improvement activity at NANO, which included the gathering of defect and interrupt data. The data was now available for analysis, which I conducted and sent the results back to the quality manager.

We then conducted a follow up phone call where we discussed the findings. I partitioned my findings into 6 major categories of "escaping defects" which we discussed on the phone. By "escaping defects" I mean defects that escaped NANO's internal testing and were not discovered until the customer was using the product.

Six common defect categories and solutions

The following are my comments during the phone call with the quality manager with respect to each of the six categories. From these comments you can gain a good idea of what many of the NANO team members viewed as the cause of the defects escaping their own testing and not being found until the customer was using the product. You can also get a sense of my initial thoughts on each defect category. Later in this story I will explain more about how we dealt with each of the categories.

Category 1– Design

Comment:

When I hear,

"We did not think through all the potential impacts,"

and the problem is categorized as a "design issue", I think, ok, I get that, but I have also heard developers complain by saying,

"Our product is very complex and many developers do not know all the potential impacts".

So to me this means that categorizing this escape purely as a design issue isn't necessarily sufficient to help us reduce these types of escapes in the future.

Category 2– Requirements

Comment:

When I hear,

"We didn't get all the requirements so we had to make assumptions,"

this leads me to ask,

"Do developers know when it is appropriate to make assumptions and proceed to work the ticket versus the option they have to reject the ticket as not ready to be worked?"

During this conversation I went on to ask,

"If they do decide to make assumptions are there others who they should alert, or discuss their assumptions with, and do they know this?"

Category 3– Legacy Requirements

Comment:

When I hear,

"This was a new use case never used before,"

it causes me to ask,

"Who is responsible to verify new use cases?"

Category 4– Test

Comment:

When I hear,

"Testers don't understand the technical limitations of the system,"

I ask,

"Are the technical limitations documented somewhere?"

Category 5– Code

Comment:

When I hear,

"This was sloppy coding,"

it leads me to ask,

"Why didn't we catch this in unit testing?"

Category 6– Developer decision to make a change

Comment:

When I hear,

"The developer decided to make a change because... [fill in the blank here with many possible reasons],"

it leads me to ask,

"Why did the developer make this decision and was it related to a clear problem reported by a customer?"

Stepping Back

When you step back and look at these categories of defects (and I realize you are only getting a short glimpse into them) I would bet that many of you can see how most, if not all, could be reduced to the basics of planning fundamental software engineering activities, and then using your plan.

Thinking a little deeper about how to reduce these categories of defects

But I realized just telling the team they need to plan better, and to use[4] their plan would not help their situation. They needed to actually see in a hands-on way where their planning and execution of their plan was falling short. And they needed to see in a hands-on way where they should be observing their own behavior, learning from that behavior, and then improving their plan and the execution of their plan everyday based on what they learned.

---

[4]By the phrase "use their plan" I mean do what it says, and update it as the team learns more

As I was thinking about all this, I also recalled that we had conducted a similar exercise at NANO a few years back with a different group within the same organization, and so I asked the quality manager:

"Did any performance improvement ever come out of that previous improvement activity we conducted a few years ago?"

And she replied,

"No."

I then asked,

"Why do you think that was the case?"

She replied,

"Because all we did was gather and analyze defects, construct a Pareto chart, and reach a conclusion on root causes. Then we updated our process documents, and our formal classroom training on how to solve the root cause which we determined to be poor elicitation of requirements. Unfortunately, people don't read process documents, and many can't connect our formal training to their real job. So we never affected their behavior."

An upside down approach to reduce common escaping defects

I replied,

"Exactly. So let's conduct this improvement effort differently. Let's not spend so much time writing our report, explaining the root cause of these defects, and updating the process documents and the formal classroom training. Let's first work with the teams, coaching them on the job specifically related to their behavior and how they might operate differently to

improve their performance. We need to do this to prove that our recommendations can indeed improve performance before we spend more effort describing what we think the team members should be doing and teaching them in the classroom. Then—once we know it works– we can confidently write up and train what the team is doing that we know works because we proved it first! This will make it much easier for us to convince other team members to read and use the "defined process" because there will be team members who can support us in our claims that this will actually help improve their performance on their projects."

The quality manager at NANO agreed. I could sense her frustration with the efforts we had conducted in the past and our failure to gain positive results that provided any significant real performance improvement.

We now had a plan to work more closely with the team members, coach them on the job, and prove that the improvements would produce higher performance. And we would do this before we spent any significant effort documenting improved processes, checklists, and formal training material.

In the next section I will share what happened in a few of the subsequent coaching sessions so you understand how we helped NANO improve their performance by working closely with team members in the areas we had discussed on the phone call.

Category 1– Design

"We did not think through all the potential impacts"

NANO has a single product, but their product can be viewed as two distinct sub-products that work closely together. They also have two distinct teams that work on each sub-product.

When I was on site at NANO I had a discussion with Jed, the technical lead for one of the sub-products. Jed has deep knowledge of his sub-product having been involved in its original design and implementation many years ago.

During the discussion I asked Jed and his manager Steve what they felt was working well, and what wasn't working so well on the project. What was interesting was that Jed's manager, Steve, said peer reviews were working well, while Jed actually called out peer reviews as something specific that was not working well.

After digging a little deeper I discovered that Steve felt peer reviews were working well because they were being done, while Jed felt peer reviews were not working well because they weren't being done well. In other words, from Jed's perspective many issues that should have been caught in peer reviews were escaping and not being discovered until much later, often by the customer after delivery.

I asked Jed if he knew why this was happening and he said that he knew what to look for in a peer review, but that many of the less experienced developers did not. When I pressed him to explain more he said he didn't know how to explain what he looked for and he admitted that a lot of it was related to his intimate product knowledge acquired from years of working with the product. This didn't surprise me as I have heard similar stories from other experienced technical developers.

I then suggested to Jed that he and I sit down and talk. I believed I could "pick his brain" and possibly come up with a useful set of peer review checklist items that we could then share with the team. This could potentially improve the way his sub-product team conducted peer reviews. You will learn more about the results of this personal coaching session with respect to code peer reviews later in the book.

While NANO's product provides great value to their customer, part of the problem they face is that both sub-products are so large and complicated that few developers understand all the potential impacts of a change. Just telling developers they need to "think through all potential impacts" isn't very useful. I wanted to learn more to see if there was something more practical we could do.

From discussions with NANO team members I learned that there are a few key developers that were recognized experts in certain areas of the product. I also learned that there are certain key areas of both sub-products that are known for being "trouble spots". I had seen similar situations in other organizations.

The idea we came up with was to develop a list that could be used by all team members to remind them when making a change to known "trouble spots." The list would also contain the names of key people to contact with questions. A similar strategy had proven effective at NORO.

Upside Down Principle Ten:

 Traditional thinking: Developers need to think-through all potential impacts to ensure their design is complete.

Clarifying thought: Developers need to know where the "trouble spots" are and who the experts are that can help.

Category 2– Requirements

"We didn't get all the requirements so we had to make assumptions"

When I hear this common cause of latent defects escaping to customers, I ask,

"Do developers know when to just make assumptions and proceed, and when they should reject a ticket as not ready?"

When I asked this question at NANO the response I got was,

"I can't reject a ticket. My manager always tells me, just make the best assumptions you can. That is all we have time to do."

When I asked the quality manager the following question,

"Do they know what else to do when they do make assumptions?"

I was digging to see if they knew enough to alert someone of the associated risk, and possibly get some action going, such as triggering the test team to take a harder look before agreeing the problem was solved.

While it is understood that under schedule pressures often certain assumptions must be made, sometimes just taking a small amount of time to talk to a peer, or subject matter expert, with a little more knowledge can be the difference between getting it right, and missing the mark.

Furthermore, when assumptions do need to be made those assumptions should be documented in a place that is visible to the testers. This can trigger appropriate additional testing reducing the risk of latent defects.

⚷ Upside Down Principle Eleven:

 Traditional thinking: If you don't have all the requirements you need, just make the best assumptions.

 Clarifying thought: If you don't have all the requirements, know who to talk to before making any assumptions.

Category 3– Legacy Requirements

"This was a new use case never used before"

This may seem like a strange cause of escaping defects. However, when you have a large complicated legacy system that has been used for years, often customers don't start using certain capabilities that have supposedly been in the system and tested until years after they were developed and released. When I hear this kind of explanation for a latent defect, I ask:

"Is it clear who is responsible to verify new use cases never used before?"

When I asked this question at NANO the answer I received was,

"The code was written a long time ago so we don't know if it was ever tested. The customer just started using this feature with our latest release."

When I heard this response I asked,

"Did anyone know that the customer was going to start using these new features, and if so could the testers have been alerted that this was an area we should have been doing more regression testing?"

Upside Down Principle Twelve:

 <u>Traditional thinking</u>: Once a requirement/use case has been accepted by the customer the team can be confident that their software works as intended.

<u>Clarifying thought</u>: Customers sometimes don't use certain capabilities until later releases when you may unexpectedly learn what doesn't work.

Category 4—Test

"Testers don't understand the technical limitations of the system"

When I heard this cause of a latent defect I asked,

"Are the technical limitations documented somewhere so testers can learn?"

Of course the common answer to this one is,

"No. What documentation does exist is old and out of date and so no one trusts it."

When I heard this, my response was similar to my response described earlier to the situation with Jed and peer reviews. I asked,

"Can't we at least create a list of the technical experts who know the systems limitations so the testers know who to talk to when they have a question? And shouldn't we at least start to improve the documentation to make it usable?"

Upside Down Principle Thirteen:

 Traditional thinking: You need to read the system documentation to understand how the software works.

 Clarifying thought: Often teams don't trust the system documentation because it isn't kept up to date.

Category 5—Code

"This was sloppy coding"

When I heard this cause of a latent defect I asked,

"Why didn't someone catch this during unit testing?"

What is interesting about this situation is that whenever I would mention "unit testing" developers at NANO would say,

"We don't unit test."

My first thought was, this is clearly an area where NANO can improve. But I wanted to first understand more, so I then asked,

"Why don't you unit test?"

The most common response was,

"Because our product doesn't lend itself to unit testing."

I couldn't understand why any software product couldn't be unit tested so I kept digging and after a deeper discussion the problem became clear.

There was a misunderstanding related to what they thought I meant when I used the phrase "unit test". The developers were thinking "automated unit tests" or "standalone unit tests". What I meant was whatever testing a developer does before saying the ticket is "done".

Once I understood this misunderstanding it reminded me of some lessons we had learned with respect to low level testing at NORO. As an example, one developer at NORO told me that many of the tickets he would be assigned to work on were not clear with respect to exactly what the problem was, or under what conditions the problem occurred. Therefore he had to make an assumption about the problem which in turn meant he didn't have a clear definition of what "done" meant. It is worth noting that this type of problem could be viewed as a sub-category of the second category of defect escapes (e.g. had to make assumptions).

What is important to understand is how this type of problem can lead to missing the real intent of the problem report and failure to conduct adequate low level testing. He then showed me an example that he was currently working on. He was about to close the ticket saying it was done leaving it at that because he didn't know what else to do. Right there I asked him,

"Do you know who wrote the ticket? Can you call him and ask him to tell you more about the situation?"

He replied,

"I tried to call the person who wrote the ticket, but he hasn't returned my call. I am getting pressure to finish."

I then said,

"Why not add a note that says what you did, and you are concerned that you didn't have more time to test the change in other configurations. You might also suggest to the tester some other conditions to test the change."

Stepping Back Again

Please note that this conversation may seem to be suggesting something that should be an obvious thing to do. However, under pressure many developers just don't take the time to think about these things. This is one reason why we need on the job coaching– to remind practitioners of the options they have right at the point where a decision needs to be made.

What I want to emphasize here is that the greatest value of

coaching is the fact that the coach is right there observing the situation when the team member is facing a specific situation and has a question. Or maybe the developer doesn't realize a question should be asked or other options exist.

Upside Down Principle Fourteen:

 Traditional thinking: If developers are formally trained in programming and unit testing techniques, we can be confident their work will be high quality.

Clarifying thought: Even when developers follow good programming and testing techniques there are situations when they know there is higher probability of escaping defects.

Category 6– Developer decision to make a change

"The developer decided to make a change because..(fill in many possible reasons..)"

When I hear this reason being given for a latent defect I ask,

"What motivated the developer to make this change?"

And

"Did a customer report a problem?"

And

"Did the developer see a potential problem and was trying to avoid it?"

And

"Did the developer weigh the risk of not making a change at all versus the risk of this change causing more serious unintended consequences?"

Sometimes developers just see things that look wrong and quickly make a change to fix a potential problem. But developers should ask a few questions before moving forward with any change that is not motivated by a clear problem reported by a customer. For example, they should always ask,

"What is the risk in making this change?"

And

"Are there likely potential negative side-effects that I can't foresee right now?"

And

"How serious are those consequences in comparison to the problem I am trying to fix right now?"

Upside Down Principle Fifteen:

 Traditional thinking: Whenever a developer sees a potential problem in the software, a change should be made to address the potential problem.

Clarifying thought: Some defects are better never fixed.

What is the point in discussing the six categories of "escaping defects" highlighted in this story?

What we have just discussed are all examples that demonstrate how traditional thinking on common causes of "escaping defects" can often miss the mark when it comes to helping practitioners improve their performance. It also demonstrates how digging deeper by asking key questions, as an on-the-job coach, can generate more practical solutions than what we traditionally often teach through formal classroom training.

It is worth highlighting the fact that some of the proposed solutions just discussed to handle common "escaping defects" may appear to be upside down from common long held beliefs. As an example, the situation in our sixth category where the right decision could be to choose not to fix a defect at all because of the risk of introducing a more serious defect.

Consciously choosing not to fix a defect is counter to what many of us have been taught. This kind of thinking has proven to work effectively in many real project situations, but not necessarily all. This is an important observation because as a coach you must always be conscious of the fact that what works in one situation, can often spell disaster in another.

Another benefit of working closely with practitioners as an on-the-job coach is that you can often observe areas where the practitioner needs reinforcement of fundamentals. Sometimes the points that need reinforcement may seem simple and obvious to you. However, it is common for less experienced practitioners to miss such points because they are too close to the problem, or just moving fast to meet a deadline.

Another advantage of working as an on-the-job coach is the ability to observe activities first hand. This allows you to periodically step back and assess whether or not the practices being used are being applied correctly and actually helping to improve performance.

When we develop processes based on industry best practices alone and deploy them only through formal classroom training apart from real project activities we miss this important opportunity for feedback, verification and improvement. This lesson applies to programming and testing, as well as all skills and competencies needed in software development. Hence, we can generalize upside down principle #14 as follows.

Upside Down Principle Sixteen:

 <u>Traditional thinking</u>: Training your team in a formal classroom setting is the best way to ensure your team will have the skills and competencies they need to produce high quality results.

<u>Clarifying thought</u>: On-the-job coaching can often help more that classroom training when it comes to helping practitioners recognize the proper action they should take in specific situations.

An upside down approach to measurement

In the first story in this book I questioned whether or not you always need measures to improve. It has been my experience that on-the-job visible observation is often the best and most practical measure of whether or not a suggested improvement actually improves performance. When you make that visible observation I recommend you also look for a more objective measure as a cross-check and validation of what you believe you are seeing.

At NORO we did not set up a measurement system before we started making improvements, but in the second sprint the Scrum Master commented,

"I was skeptical that this new approach would actually help us. But I know we are much more productive now."

At that moment when he made this comment I challenged him by replying,

"Would you take an action to see if you can find an objective measure that could confirm what you say you know is really helping?"

The Scrum Master took the action and the next day he reported:

"I have data here that confirms we are performing at 100% higher productivity than before we started this new approach. I searched through old logs to see how many tasks we were completing per day versus how many we are doing now. We were getting at most 1 task done per day, and now we are consistently completing 2 -3 per day."

He went on to say,

"Furthermore, I had to spend a lot of time just digging through old logs to find the data before we went to the new approach, but now with the new way of tracking all our work it is simple for me to see how much work we are getting done each day and each week."

Extending Upside Down Principle Three:

<u>Traditional thinking</u>: You need to establish measures first to be sure changes lead to real performance improvement.

<u>Extended Clarifying thought</u>: Sometimes the most practical and meaningful measures can be identified right at the point where you know you have improved your performance.

Summary Upside Down Principles 10, 11, 12, 13, 14, 15, 16

<u>Principle Ten:</u> *Developers need to think-through all potential impacts to ensure their design is complete*

<u>Extended clarifying thought:</u> Just telling developers to "think-through all potential impacts" is sometimes just not practical. With many complicated legacy systems often developers do not have sufficient product knowledge to understand all potential change impacts. Creating a list of common "trouble spots" and contact experts can help mitigate the risk of software breakage due to unanticipated side-effects of changes.

<u>Principle Eleven:</u> *If you don't have all the requirements you need, just make the best assumptions*

<u>Extended clarifying thought:</u> If you don't have all the requirements you need, first talk to a peer or subject matter expert with a little more knowledge to ensure your assumptions are valid. Second, document assumptions in a place that is visible to the testers and anyone else with a need to know.

<u>Principle Twelve:</u> *Once a requirement/use case has been accepted by the customer the team can be confident that their software works as intended*

<u>Extended clarifying thought:</u> It is not uncommon, especially on large complicated legacy systems, for certain capabilities not to be used when initially released, but then used by customers in later releases. Therefore teams need to work closely with key stakeholders to understand their needs and vision for each upcoming product release.

<u>Principle Thirteen:</u> *You need to read the system documentation*

to understand how the software works

Extended clarifying thought: Often teams cannot trust system documentation because it isn't kept up to date, but this doesn't alleviate the need for key team members to understand the technical limitations of the system. This need is often best addressed by ensuring team members know other team members who have the critical knowledge they may need. And if the system documentation is not trusted, do something to make it, at least, a little bit better right now.

Principle Fourteen: *If developers are formally trained in programming and unit testing techniques, we can be confident their work will be high quality*

Extended clarifying thought: While most defects should be caught by developers during low level testing activities, there are many common situations that arise where developers know there is higher likelihood of "escaped" defects. In these cases developers should take the time to communicate associated risks and potential need for additional testing. One proven good practice is to add checklists to remind developers of such common situations, and to pay particular attention in these situations to ensure the work is adequately broken down with a clear definition of what "done" means. The more specific the checklists can be the better, such as reminders of past product trouble spots.

Principle Fifteen: *Whenever a developer sees a potential problem in the software, a change should be made to address the potential problem*

Extended clarifying thought: While we want to avoid potential problems, anytime you make a change to the software you add risk of unintended consequences. Therefore this risk should always be assessed against the significance of the potential problem before proceeding with a change.

Principle Sixteen: *Training your team in a formal classroom setting is the best way to ensure your team will have the skills and competencies they need to produce high quality results*

Extended clarifying thought: While formal classroom training focusing on industry best practices can help, on-the-job coaching can often help practitioners more from the perspective of learning how to apply industry best practices in their own project situation.

Story Four: Accidentally Figuring Out a Better Way

A phrase I started using recently is "thinking patterns." The idea of a "thinking pattern" is based on identifying a common scenario, or situation that often happens and explaining it through a story like many of those I have shared in this book. You then extract the essentials of the story and add in key questions, tips and warnings to help people think-through the story, or some version of the story that better fits their own situation. I call this a "thinking pattern" because the questions, tips and warnings stimulate you to think-through the situation helping you arrive at the best decision given your own specific situation. The more you use this technique the more you develop effective patterns of thinking.

Discovering "Thinking Patterns"

Let me now explain how I discovered the idea of thinking patterns. Many years ago I was giving a workshop at one of my client sites training the participants in processes I had helped them develop. This was back when I used to conduct training the traditional way in a formal classroom atmosphere with literally hundreds of slides.

In this case, which wasn't unusual back then, we had spent months in working groups defining, reviewing, refining and getting all the processes approved. Now we were rolling out the training of all the new processes to the entire organization.

At the time I was teaching the participants their new project planning process using my five step approach to planning which I referred to as the "what", "who", "when", "how" and "how much". I thought I had simplified planning with this approach hitting just the essentials that all good plans needed to have.

During a break in the training one of the attendees came up to me and said,

"This all sounds good, but I don't know how I can use these principles in the fog of war of my real project."

When we got back from the break I turned to the same participant and said,

"Joe, could you share with the group the problem you have that you were describing to me during the break?"

And Joe responded,

"Sure. That's easy. I can't control my day. As soon as I arrive in the morning I am fighting one fire after the next. So there is no way I can plan and then follow the plan."

Immediately a different participant interrupted saying,

"Wow! It sounds like you work in my company. My day is exactly the same."

And soon everyone was engaged in the discussion sharing different but similar situations, and asking each other questions, as well as offering ideas that each had used to cope with this common situation. As this was happening I stepped back and let the conversation go, and started jotting down on a big white pad key points that were coming out of the discussion.

This was the start of a change I gradually made to how I conducted process training for my clients. As these workshops continued I started encouraging more and more of these personal sharing experiences. I still taught process basics, but over time I started spending less and less time on process fundamentals, and more and more time encouraging the group to share their own experiences, warnings and tips on how to deal with common related situations.

The reason I moved my workshop in this direction is because this is what the participants needed to be more effective at their job. The basic process definitions were still needed, but they didn't provide sufficient help to the participants when it came to "**how to**" actually implement those processes in a real project environment. The stories gave life to the processes, and provided the insights into how you actually do certain activities, such as planning, in the real environment practitioners often must live within.

Simulating the real work environment

In a sense, what we were doing in these workshops was creating a simulation of the real workplace and then discussing options related to "**how to**" handle those situations. I found this approach to be more effective than just teaching the steps of a process in the workshop.

But even this approach to coaching has its limitation because while we are creating an environment to teach that is closer to the real environment, we are still in a controlled formal educational environment. The best place to really coach is in a real live project environment where real decisions have to be made. We saw multiple examples of how this works back in story two and story three earlier in this book where I worked directly with the NORO and NANO teams helping them with the real issues they faced on the job.

Let me say a little bit more with regard to how this type of coaching differs from what I previously did with my clients and how we evolved it to get even closer to the real challenges practitioners face each day on the job.

From simulation to "on the job" coaching

On one of my subsequent trips to NANO to help the team, the quality assurance manager and I wanted to make sure everyone understood that I wasn't coming to deliver my usual formal workshop training. I used to show up for 3-4 day workshops with literally hundreds of slides. This time I would bring no slides. And this time I would work with practitioners right on the job helping them with their current challenges— not talking about theoretical classroom scenarios. Now we would discuss the real situations people were facing on their real project and we would discuss those situations right when they needed to make project decisions.

This approach also turned out to be more appealing to the managers at NANO because the team was always under the gun to solve the latest crisis. Any time I showed up and we had to schedule formal classroom training it was viewed as an "interrupt" that was taking valuable time away from the team's solving their current critical issues– which they always seemed to have. Now let me share some examples of what happened during a few of these on-the-job coaching sessions along with some coaching tips.

Coaching tip #1: Coaching developers to connect their responsibilities to what they do each day

A good example of coaching a practitioner in their real responsibilities can be found in one of my sessions with Jed.

Jed is one of the technical leads at NANO. He was the senior experienced technical lead/developer that knew more than anyone else about one of the two key sub-products at NANO (story three).

When we gathered the interrupt data in hopes of reducing interrupts to Jed's day we discovered that many of the so called "interrupts" were actually things Jed should have been able to plan for. Examples of what Jed had viewed as interrupts were things like being asked to participate in a review or a design discussion, preparing for a patch release, and supporting the installation of a new tool. Part of the reason Jed viewed these as interrupts was because he was also a developer. He had taken on a role as technical leader, but he also took on actual development tasks.

Because Jed had taken on fairly large development tasks he tended to view his leadership tasks as interrupts since they often caused him to get further behind in his development work.

One of the techniques I now use when coaching practitioners like Jed is to ask them to make a list of all their responsibilities as they see their job. Then I ask them to make a different list of things they feel they are often asked to do, but they don't feel are actually part of their responsibilities.

Upside Down Principle Seventeen:

 Traditional thinking: Training people in a classroom setting in roles and responsibilities is the best way to ensure they know their responsibilities and can carry them out.

Clarifying thought: Coaching practitioners in their responsibilities during real project situations can be more effective than classroom training at helping them carry out those responsibilities.

The value of helping team members reflect on their responsibilities

Going through an exercise, such as the one just described, that stimulates team members to reflect on their responsibilities can generate great discussion. I have also found it is far more beneficial to the practitioner than just conducting the traditional roles and responsibilities type of training often seen in formal classroom settings. People will read a list of responsibilities that have been given to them in a formal training session. However, too often they will fail to internalize the list by asking how the list of responsibilities actually matches up with the way their typical day goes.

What usually results from this type of exercise is an agreement that some of the activities previously viewed as interrupts really are activities they should expect and should be planning. This is because they are part of their responsibilities. For example, a technical leader should be planning on reviewing the work of others and providing comments. This takes effort, and time away from other potential activities.

If, by the time we are done with the exercise, there are activities that are still on the interrupt list that we agree are not part of their responsibilities it usually results in an action item. This action often leads to a follow-on discussion, often with others in the organization who should be involved with those activities. The best part of this exercise is that it generates valuable discussion and almost always leads to agreed-to actionable improvements.

Coaching tip #2: Coaching technical leaders to recognize when they should "do work" and when they should "coach others in doing work".

One of the most insightful pieces of information we learned from the exercise with Jed was that, although he agreed reviewing code was part of his responsibilities, he was not just reviewing code and then coaching the junior developers in how to fix the problem. He was actually going in and fixing the code himself which was taking even more of his limited valuable time. When I asked him why he was actually fixing the code, he replied,

"Because often it is just faster for me to fix it than to try to explain how to fix it."

I replied,

"But when you fix it, Jed, the junior developer doesn't learn anything, and so you may have fixed this one problem, but the organization didn't get better. If you help the junior people, over time your work load will lessen and the overall

organization benefits."

What is important to understand from this discussion is that Jed understood this when explained to him. However, the most valuable time to remind Jed is on-the-job right when he is facing this type of situation. This is because even though he knows it is true that he should be coaching and not fixing the junior developer's mistakes, it is very difficult for people to break long established habits.

Like Jed, many of us need a coach that is right there on-the-job to remind us of the proper action to take right when a common situation occurs where our tendency might be to make a poor decision.

Coaching tip #3: Improving the code review skills of less experienced developers

I asked Jed's manager if I could sit with Jed and just observe while he was reviewing another junior developer's code that had been checked into the repository. I wanted to see exactly how he went about doing the review, what he looked for, and when exactly he engaged with the developer. Part of the reason I wanted to see this was because Jed had previously said to me,

"A lot of the junior developers don't know how to do a code review."

When I asked Jed what he looks for when doing a peer review he replied,

"I don't know how to explain to junior developers how I go about doing a code review."

By sitting down with Jed right when he was doing a code review I could ask him what he was thinking at key points in time. This would allow me to capture key thoughts he was having so we could write them down to share with less experienced developers.

A lot of organizations realize they need to do code peer reviews, but they don't realize the importance in having peer review guidelines that capture how your best peer reviewers review code and/or other products.

As an example, when I see peer review guidelines that are general in nature and used for any product, I suggest that the organization consider more specific checklists oriented toward specific products, such as code or test cases.

Upside Down Principle Eighteen:

 <u>Traditional thinking</u>: Training team members in general peer review guidelines is the best way to ensure effective reviews are conducted.

<u>Clarifying thought</u>: Product-specific checklists are often more effective than general peer review guidelines at helping team members conduct high quality reviews that surface common problems.

Why product specific checklists help performance

Part of the reason I suggest to my clients that they develop product specific checklists is because many software developers think because they know how to program that they must know how to peer review code. But what I learned from working with Jed and other experienced programmers indicates this is not always true.

For example, I learned from watching Jed conduct a code review that he relies on his understanding of the overall architecture of a software system and his experience related to where the product has exhibited problems in the past. He knows he has limited time when conducting a code review so he relies on his experience to tell him where to focus his attention to get the most value out of his available time. Jed also knows, as do most experienced programmers, that past problem areas in the code are the most likely areas for future problems as well which helps Jed make better peer review decisions.

I now suggest when working with experienced developers who are reviewing code that they bring less experienced developers in right from the start. This allows the less experienced developer to learn faster how an experienced developer conducts a code review.

Upside Down Principle Nineteen:

 Traditional thinking: Anyone who can code, can peer review code.

Clarifying thought: Peer reviewing code requires a different skill than writing code.

How inexperienced practitioners learn outside the classroom

What I have observed happening when experienced developers work closely with inexperienced developers reviewing code is that the experienced developer– who may say they don't know how to explain how they review code– just starts talking about the product. This leads the experienced developer to explain what they are looking for as the junior developer listens.

What I find is that most experienced developers really can explain what they are looking for once you initiate this type of collaborative code review. In one recent case I observed a junior developer taking plenty of notes as the experienced developer explained his thinking. After this review the junior developer commented,

"That was well worth my time. I learned a lot and the next time I make a change in that part of the code I will be thinking very differently."

It is not uncommon for experienced busy senior developers to feel this kind of collaborative peer review is inefficient as they believe they could do the review faster alone. But it has been my experience that the coaching value that results from these peer review exchanges pays back quickly as it rapidly improves the peer review competency of less experienced developers. This approach, in the long run, helps to reduce the experienced developer's work load as they can rely on higher quality reviews being conducted throughout the project.

Coaching tip #4: Guiding experienced developers in becoming better coaches

In Jed's case he eventually realized he needed to take on fewer coding tasks himself, and conduct more collaborative reviews with the developers. Jed also realized that he needed to take the time to explain the consequences of the immediate change they were making to the code at the time, and what else to look for to reduce the likelihood of unintended consequences. This of course took more of Jed's time. However, this is also how Jed learned how much time his responsibilities associated with his leadership position required. As a result of these collaborative code review sessions Jed learned how to develop more accurate estimates of the time his leadership responsibilities required.

NANO had defined and documented roles and responsibilities well before I conducted these on-the-job coaching sessions. An example of a few of the responsibilities at NANO of a technical leader that had been documented and trained in a formal classroom setting for years prior to my on-the-job coaching sessions are:

· Participate in reviews of designs and implementation

· Provide technical mentoring

· Assist in definition and set up of the engineering environment

But just providing to a technical leader in a classroom environment a list of their responsibilities has proven not to be the most effective way to help technical leaders like Jed do their job. Coaching on-the-job right when someone has to make a decision can be an eye-opening experience as it connects their real responsibilities to their real day to day job.

Coaching tip #5: Sharing the benefits of code reviews (beyond finding defects) to motivate better performance

Benefit #1 of code peer reviews beyond finding defects

At NORO we teamed people up to conduct code reviews because we viewed peer reviewing of code as having two purposes. One purpose is to conduct the peer review and find defects. The other purpose was to create a learning opportunity so we had backups in case key people became ill, or unexpectedly left the company.

This dual purpose approach provides multiple benefits, especially in small organizations that often have trouble finding the right individual with time and the right expertise to conduct a code peer review. First, it tends to improve the code peer review quality because the person doing the review feels they need to really understand the system since they might have to take over the work. Second, it helps to keep morale high as most team members like to be given opportunities to learn new things which can help them grow their competency. But even beyond these benefits there is another benefit that few organizations think about.

Benefit #2 of code peer reviews beyond finding defects

As we improved the peer reviews and low level testing at both NORO and NANO, we also helped team members learn to estimate better. This benefit may not be obvious so let me explain how this occurred.

We observed improved estimating occurring at both NORO and NANO without directly coaching the team members in estimation best practices. We determined that this improvement happened as a positive side-effect of our code peer review improvements. By reminding the team members that both low level testing and code peer reviews were activities that were part of their normal responsibilities it brought an increased awareness of this activity to each developer. Team members consequently began thinking more about the time they spent on low level testing and code peer reviews which helped their overall work task estimating. It didn't take long before the culture at both organizations changed with regard to no longer viewing code peer reviews as "interrupts" and recognizing this activity as a natural part of their job that needed to be taken into consideration when making task effort and schedule commitments.

Coaching tip #6: Guiding developers to recognize situations where they should ask for help

There is another cultural team aspect of peer reviews that is worth discussing. I recall when I was a young programmer coming into work on a weekend to rewrite a large section of code because I felt I had made a big mistake with my design. I was afraid to let my technical leader know what I had done so I did not tell him and I didn't even let him know that I had come in on that weekend. I was afraid what my technical leader would think of me and of my programming skills.

Since my early programming years, I have heard a number of similar stories from other junior programmers. One new developer told me that he had been given a mentor when he came in to his company, but the mentor never had time to help him. The point of this story is that we need to help our junior developers learn sound programming skills and how to peer review. However, we also need to guide them to understand when it is ok to ask for help, and we need to make sure when they ask for help that help is available.

Coaching tip #7: Guiding testers in developing and maintaining a regression test suite

Let me now share a story related to how I helped NORO testers improve their regression testing, and how I was able to share this experience to help NANO with a similar, but different, challenge.

Because NORO had no regression test suite when I first started working with them, I provided a test case template to their product owner. I also suggested that he get started by writing up the tests he felt should be run for the current sprint, and then every sprint add more test cases. Because the task of writing all the regression tests that NORO felt they needed seemed overwhelming to them, I suggested that they just get started, and plan to do a little during each sprint.

Any regression tests would be better that none, which is what they had when I started helping them. I also explained that their test suite would keep getting better every sprint as long as they just kept updating the tests a little each sprint and continued working to make them better with whatever time they had available.

I asked the product owner to send me his first draft of the regression test suite so I could review it and provide feedback. When I read the test cases the product owner had developed my first thought was that I couldn't run them from the information he provided. However, the more important question was, could the NORO tester run them? So I asked the tester, Jack, if he thought there was enough information for him to run the test suite.

Some people at NORO first argued that test cases should be written at a level of detail where anyone can run them. This was an idea they had previously learned when working at a large defense company. However, what needs to be considered is the fact that this approach often leads to detailed lengthy step by step procedures which takes a great deal more effort than what might be needed by someone who is experienced with a given software product. And once these lengthy detailed step by step test procedures have been written they take considerable effort to maintain as small changes to the software going forward are more likely to impact the test steps. Therefore, when deciding the level of detail of test cases you should ask a few questions before deciding, such as,

"If Jack can run the tests because he knows the system, what is the risk if he leaves the company or becomes ill, and we have to use someone else to run the tests?"

The president at NORO said that he wanted to be able to use new personnel to do testing. However, after discussing the effort involved to develop and maintain such detailed tests, we agreed that any new tester would need training with a more experienced tester before being expected to run the regression tests on his or her own. This allowed us to develop the test cases in a more lean cost effective way.

Upside Down Principle Twenty:

 Traditional thinking: Test procedures (or any other procedures) need to be written at the step by step detailed level so that less experienced personnel can use them.

Clarifying thought: Balance the cost of developing and maintaining a detailed process versus relying to some degree on the skill level of the practitioner using the process.

Balancing the tradeoffs

This is an example where organizations need to balance the trade-off between the cost of developing and maintaining detailed step by step regression test procedures (or any other procedures) and the cost of training new personnel (e.g. testers).

I shared my story from my NORO regression testing coaching experience with NANO personnel. NANO was experiencing similar difficulties in regard to effective regression testing, but NANO's immediate issues were a bit different. In NANO's case the immediate issue revolved around miscommunication between developers and testers.

After some discussion at NANO we decided to pair developers with testers during part of their testing process to improve the communication and effectiveness of the testing. In their situation they decided there wasn't value in providing more detailed step by step regression tests. The thinking was that by getting the testers and developers to talk more they would avoid the common miscommunications that appeared to be allowing defects to escape to the customer.

This simple example demonstrates how teams often learn the value of collaboration and communication over extensive documentation. It also demonstrates how teams achieve the real goal they seek by modifying their agreed to way of working based on their own specific project situation.

Coaching tip #8: Guiding your agile/Scrum team in the pros and cons of choosing different sprint lengths

There were some interesting revelations that resulted from the informal discussions at both NORO and NANO with respect to sprint length. At both organizations I asked,

"Do we have all the priority work on the sprint backlog that will need to be done during the next sprint?"

It turned out that NORO was better able to answer this question because they were using two week sprints. This is because it was easier for them to forecast what was on the horizon over the next two weeks than it was for NANO who was using 30 day sprints. The advantage that NORO discovered using two week sprints was that it made it easier to eliminate the "pop up" unexpected tasks due to the interrupt driven culture. This was because people only needed to wait at most two weeks to get a new critical need addressed. When you are conducting 30 day sprints, as NANO was, often managers do not want to wait a month to get their issue worked. Therefore, changing the interrupt culture at NANO was more difficult. This is one of the reasons why measuring interrupts was chosen at NANO as we saw in story one.

When you are using 30 day sprints there is also a tendency not to break the tasks down as fine as when using two week sprints. The goal we set both at NANO and NORO was to try to get all tasks broken down to 4-16 hour tasks. This is because it helps team members see and report progress approximately every 1-2 days during the daily standups as work is being completed. At NANO this was more challenging due at least in part to the longer sprint length and the culture of not always breaking the work down to the level where progress could be seen at a daily level.

Reflection

What I want the reader to understand about the coaching stories in this chapter is that I had for years been helping clients by collecting and analyzing data and then documenting the results in reports, and providing training to my clients in a formal classroom setting. Although we would periodically analyze data from real projects and implement corresponding improvements to processes and training, we struggled to find significant resulting measurable performance improvements.

Finally I suggested to one client after the analysis of some interrupt and defect data that I should just go to their location and work directly with their teams in their real work environment. The idea was that by talking to their practitioners in a real work environment I was more likely to see things that we were missing by just analyzing data and training them in industry best practices in a formal classroom setting.

These discussions led at first to a few small changes where we could rapidly see measurable improvement. The next step was to gradually change the culture by making simple changes part of everyone's normal routine. The results led to clear and significant measurable improvements over surprisingly short periods of time.

Examples of measurable performance improvement

Examples where we were able to rapidly achieve measurable performance improvements with small changes include helping practitioners understand their responsibilities, helping practitioners plan their time considering those responsibilities, and helping them reduce the sense of always reacting to fire-drills. All of these seemingly "small changes" led to improved predictability by considering past performance and responsibilities.

A good example of predicting better by considering past performance and responsibilities can be seen with the task of setting up a test environment. This task had previously been viewed as an unplanned interrupt at NANO, but when we discussed it a technical leader realized he should have known this activity was coming and he could have planned for it.

Industry "best practices" and "lessons learned"

It is also worth noting that during these informal coaching sessions I did share "best practices" and "lessons learned" that were common across the industry. Those lessons and best practices were useful to NANO and NORO, but they were only useful to stimulate a discussion related to each organization's specific situation. We started with industry proven checklists. However, we made many improvements to checklists based on specific issues that were hurting the performance of each organization. For examples of improved unit test checklists at NORO refer back to Story Two. The way of working that evolved at both NANO and NORO, while there were similarities to what other organizations did, was unique to each organization.

Summary Upside Down Principles 17, 18, 19, 20

Principle Seventeen: *Training people in a classroom setting in roles and responsibilities is the best way to ensure they know their responsibilities and can carry them out*

Extended clarifying thought: Coaching practitioners in their responsibilities during real project situations can be more effective than classroom training at helping them achieve the competency they need to carry out their responsibilities appropriately each day on the job.

Principle Eighteen: *Training team members in general peer review guidelines is the best way to ensure effective reviews are conducted*

Extended clarifying thought: While it is true that general peer review guidelines can be shared and used across diverse products, product-specific checklists are often more effective at helping team members learn to conduct high quality reviews that surface common problems. An example was provided earlier in this story when I explained what I learned about how Jed does peer reviews and how it ties to his knowledge of the product architecture.

Principle Nineteen: *Anyone who can code, can peer review code*

Extended clarifying thought: It takes experience and product-specific knowledge to know where to focus your peer review effort when you have limited time (and we all have limited time).

Principle Twenty: *Test procedures (or any other procedures) need to be written at the step by step detailed level so that less experienced personnel can use them*

Extended clarifying thought: It is true that step by step detailed test procedures (or any other procedure) can help to ensure less experienced personnel can apply the procedure correctly (e.g. set up and conduct tests properly). However, trade-offs should be considered balancing the cost of developing and maintaining detailed procedures versus the risk in relying to some degree on the skill level of more experienced personnel.

Story Five: Software Development in Action

The quality manager at NANO and myself had discussed the idea of my sitting in on a sprint planning session during one of my visits to their location. I had previously given the group training in Scrum and in that training I highlighted the essentials of five basic Scrum practices. In that training I also highlighted common Scrum tailoring decisions I had observed in other organizations. Some of this tailoring was effective while other tailoring had led to trouble in other organizations. I was trying to get NANO to think-through the consequences of certain common behaviors they exhibited that I felt could be hurting their performance. Let me now share a few examples related to planning.

Coaching tip #9: Keeping your team aware of how much work they can do in a day

One area related to how the NANO team did capacity planning. At the Scrum training I highlighted the fact that a good practice was to assume an actual work day was 6 or 7 hours because people need typically 1-2 hours for reading email and doing administrative tasks. The fact is that most organizations have figured out that it is unrealistic to think you can do a full 8 hours of productive task work each day. Factoring your daily capacity planning this way can help your team put realistic plans in place that they can hit more predictably.

Coaching tip #10: Helping your team understand the best work task size, and what to do when they disagree

Another best practice I shared was breaking tasks down to the 4-16 hour level. We had a good discussion on this best practice at NANO, just like we had at NORO. Although at NORO this practice was easier for the team to accept because they were doing two week sprints. The longer your sprint length the greater the temptation for teams to keep their tasks at a less granular level, as discussed in the previous story.

Also, at NANO, I heard a common belief that there were certain tasks that it just didn't make sense to break down to the 4-16 hour level. When I heard this I suggested that we should take a closer look at those tasks to see if we could characterize them so we could help other team members determine when it was ok to keep tasks at a level greater than 4-16 hours. [5]

Motivation for coaching tip #10

I found at NANO something similar going on to what I had observed in Sprint 4 at NORO. That is, when we don't adequately break the tasks down it becomes easier to take on too much work. This can lead a team to feel, after the sprint, that they failed.

As an example, at NANO a manager of one of the sub-products told me he felt his technical leaders often missed their targets. When we looked at why this might be happening we discovered the targets were vague which left the team open to having anyone say they fell short. Note here that "vague" targets are a common side-effect of teams failing to

---

[5]Refer to coaching tip #14 for more information on a specific example of the type of task NANO personnel didn't think made sense to break down to 4-16 hour and more information on how I handled this challenge in a coaching session.

adequately break their work down with clear definition of done.

As a related example, at NANO defects were often being written up in areas that were beyond the scope of what the team felt they had committed to do. This was happening because the tickets they committed to work were vague with no clear definition of done. This situation left the door open for any stakeholder to write up a ticket that went beyond what the team had interpreted as their commitment.

I had previously observed a similar pattern at NORO in Sprint 4 where I explained to the team that it was to their advantage to break the work down with clear "done" criteria. This is because it would make the success criteria clear to everyone and not leave that door open for stakeholders to push the team beyond the agreed-to scope.

An example of applying coaching tip #10

To help you understand why breaking the work down helps the team, you should understand that when you break the work down with clear definition of done, then when a stake-holder says,

"It doesn't do XYZ",

Then you can say,

"We will put XYZ on the backlog. XYZ wasn't part of our goal to do in this sprint. It wasn't part of our definition of done for any of the tickets we committed to. We hit our goal in this sprint as we showed you everything we committed to. Now we will work XYZ as part of the goal in the next sprint if you agree that is a priority."

This really changes a team's attitude. It helps the team that is working hard view their work as successful because they have a clear goal that is achieved each sprint and this creates higher morale and a more effective working environment.[6]

Coaching tip #11: Helping your team reverse the "we're always reacting to fire-drills" culture

I found at NANO that they were not putting all their work on the backlog. They used planning poker and they maintained a team story point velocity. However, they didn't adequately consider all the work that they should have been able to predict they would be asked to complete during the sprint. A specific example I heard that I mentioned in the previous story in Coaching Tip #1 was supporting the installation of a new tool.

So one simple way to change the *"we are always reacting to fire-drills"* culture, is to observe what goes on in your organization. Then predict it by planning on it. It turned out at NANO that a lot of the fire-drills could be eliminated just through better planning.

But we had to get closer observing what was happening on a typical day and observing how the team was conducting their sprint planning to understand how this improvement could help. I then coached the team in this behavior change right at the time they were committing to their sprint plan.

Upside down coaching tip #12: Another way to help your team reverse the "we're always reacting to fire-drills" culture

As another example, I told NANO team members that since they frequently found themselves with the additional un-planned effort of supporting "patch releases" they should consider discontinuing their practice of calling them "patch

---

[6]Refer to coaching tip #14 for a more concrete example related to this tip

releases", and plan on them by referring to them as "continuous delivery".

This is one of those seemingly upside down ideas, but it is one that has been proven to work. We think of a "patch release" that is unplanned as meaning we must have done something wrong. We failed. But if it is part of the plan to do continuous delivery then it can be viewed as a normal part of how the team works.

In other words, if you have a history of always doing patch releases, until you can figure out how to change that poor behavior, you should plan on it. That is, use your data that shows your recent past performance to predict future performance. But please understand that I am not saying this is all you should do. This is just a first step. See the section below on "Understanding the difference between "continuous delivery" and "interrupt patch releases" for more information on the next steps.

This can change a team's attitude and it can change an organization's culture from one of feeling like it is always reacting, to one that is continuously planning. This helps teams operate in a more predictable way.

It may sound upside down, but it works. Plan it, don't react to it. And you can stop your fire-drill culture more easily than you might think.

Understanding the difference between "continuous delivery" and "interrupt patch releases"

Now, please don't get the wrong idea because I know what I just suggested can easily be misinterpreted. When I say "plan to do continuous delivery" this doesn't mean that we plan to always react with another quick "interrupt patch release".

It means that we develop a culture of planning, doing, checking and delivering in short cycles with a sustainable pace. This is not the same as having a plan get interrupted due to an unexpected and unplanned new task that just popped up to get a patch out to a given customer in the next 24 hours.

Now, some might object to this "upside down" tip by pointing out that what I am recommending is more than just changing the name of a practice from "patch release" to "continuous delivery". In fact, this is true. It does require behavior change to stop reacting, and start to plan continuously. Developing a culture of delivering in short cycles is not easy. Continuous delivery requires a culture of breaking the work down into much smaller task sizes than what many organizations do.

However, I intentionally describe this tip in this simplified way to help your team get started down the path to improvement. Cultural improvements are best implemented in small steps. Changing the name of a practice can be a simple first step to changing the way an organization operates. Culture change is never easy. So start small. Otherwise, you may never change at all.

Coaching tip #13: General principle to keep in mind when coaching your team to plan better

When many of us were taught the fundamentals of planning we were thinking we need to plan everything upfront. Even if we didn't know enough. What we have learned is to plan shorter and more often and plan only what you know. You can still plan further out, but you plan at a higher level further out because you don't know as much. And you know your plan is more likely to change further out so you don't want to put too much effort into that further out planning because that is likely to lead to waste.

However, there is another side to planning that we all should think about when deciding how much detail should be in our plan that is captured in the next tip.

Upside down coaching tip #14: Helping your team break "uncertain work" down without wasting their time

I often hear about tasks that can't be broken down when software teams are doing new development.[7] I mentioned earlier that I heard this at NANO. The thinking is that when there is significant levels of uncertainty that we can't break the work down very far because we don't know enough to break it down. This may be accurate. But it may not. The approach I take when coaching clients facing uncertain situations is to help them learn how to plan the right level of detail, without wasted planning effort. I will explain the approach through the

"I just don't know enough common scenario".

When I hear that we,

"just don't know enough to break the work down",

I usually respond with,

"Ok, then put an analysis task in."

And then someone often says,

"Ok. We'll just do 40 hours of analysis this sprint and see where we are."

When I hear this common response I challenge them because that is a trap that leads to poor planning. I say,

---

[7]Coaching tip #14 provides a different, but similar perspective as the previous Coaching tip #10. This tip may be viewed as a specific example (e.g. uncertain work) of coaching tip #10.

"You need completion criteria so you can demonstrate what you achieved even with analysis tasks. What will done mean for this analysis task at the end of this sprint? The goal must be clear so that we can measure our success at the sprint review even with analysis tasks."

Upside Down Principle Twenty-One:

 Traditional thinking: Sometimes we just don't know enough to break the work down.

Clarifying thought: You can always create completion criteria with clear definition of done.

An example applying upside down coaching tip #14

Now let me give an example. Let's say that we are facing that situation where we have uncertainty and we feel we need to do more analysis before we can break the work down. So the next question you should ask is,

"What exactly are you going to analyze"?

If the entire analysis task is too much for one sprint, then can you identify well defined pieces of the analysis task? For example, can we agree that we will analyze sub-system x and y, but not z? Then possibly we could plan to design and code a specific small piece of x and y, and demonstrate the result. By making this plan explicitly clear, if a stakeholder starts raising issues, or writing up defects related to z, you can say,

"We didn't plan to do z this sprint. We only planned to do x and y, and we demonstrated what we said we would do."

This is the way to think and plan. You aren't planning what you don't know, but you can plan at a level where you can say what "done" means and demonstrate the results even with analysis tasks.

At worst case, if there just isn't time to do any implementation (code and test) of even a small piece to demonstrate working software, you can at least report the specific results of the pieces of your analysis completed. Then you can take credit for that work as long as it meets the agreed-to done criteria. The value of thinking this way is that your team morale will stay high because they know they have met their agreed-to commitment.

As a specific example of where thinking and planning this way could have helped, I heard in the sprint 4 review at NORO that a number of planned tasks did not get done. Specifically I heard,

"We are rolling these tasks back into the next sprint."

When we discussed in the retrospective why these tasks didn't get done we found the reason was that we got something done, but we learned more, and NORO had a stakeholder with greater depth of knowledge than the developers reviewing the product. That stakeholder commented on things that the developers just didn't understand while they were working their agreed tasks during the sprint. Since they hadn't been clear on their definition of done it left them open to criticism related to not achieving the goal of the sprint as seen by the stakeholders.

I noticed at the end of this sprint that there was a sense

among the team that the sprint had not been as successful as a number of previous sprints. The heads were a bit down because they had worked hard and they felt they had fallen short of the goal given the stakeholder's comments.

So I replied,

"This is why we need to be clear on what we are committing to. If we had said at the start of the sprint we are going to make these scenarios work and we will use these test cases as our agreed-to definition of done, then if we were able to demonstrate what we said we would do, everyone would agree the sprint was a success. Then when one of the stakeholders points out some weaknesses or added features at the sprint review we can say, 'great feedback'. We will put those features on the backlog and work them next sprint if they are high priority. This way, we can still close the backlog items we committed to because we hit our agreed-to goal. Going forward in the next sprint we can make the product better by focusing on the next items the customer is asking for during the next sprint."

Some might argue that in the scenario just described that we aren't really helping the team become more productive because they aren't actually getting any more work done. But the question you need to ask is,

Do you want higher productivity or predictable performance?

Note: Before you read this section you should be aware that my suggested answer to this question may sound upside down to you. So I just want you to be prepared.

It has been my experience that no matter how productive your team is some stakeholders will always keep pushing for more.

Stakeholders often don't know how hard a team has worked to get them the functionality they are currently reviewing. Therefore stakeholders tend to focus on what they perceive as missing, rather than what has been achieved. This can be demoralizing to a hard working team. You will always face this type of challenge with stakeholders on the productivity improvement side no matter how productive your team is.

Now let's consider what is needed for predictable performance and the benefits predictable performance can bring.

First, it is important to understand that predictable performance is closely coupled with the morale of your team, as well as the confidence of your stakeholders in the team. Being clear with what the team commits to, and then demonstrating that your team can perform predictably keeps your team's morale high, as well as the confidence of your stakeholders in the team's ability to perform. High team morale, in turn, helps the team to sustain their predictable performance into the future. Promise what you know you can do, and you will deliver predictably, and you will maintain the confidence of your stakeholders.

Now–think again– which do you want:

Higher productivity or predictable performance?

Summary Upside Down Principle 21

Principle Twenty-One: *Sometimes we just don't know enough to break the work down*

Extended clarifying thought: Even when you know you need to do more analysis because you don't know enough about the problem, you can always create completion criteria with a clear definition of done. This is the best path to predictably achieving your goals.

Story Six: Upside Down Ideas on Estimating

Often when I ask someone how long a certain activity will take I get the following kind of a response,

"I don't have a clue how long it will take me."

Actually, in most of these cases, I have learned they do have a pretty good idea how long most activities they conduct will take them. But when asked, either they don't realize they know because they never took the time to think about it, or they did think about it and they made a conscious decision to keep the answer to themselves.

The reason I know this is because when I have asked practitioners to describe the activities they conduct, and then I ask them how long each piece of a certain activity takes, they are able to provide reasonable estimates.

Why many practitioners don't like to give estimates

Even when people know the answer to the *"how long will it take you"* question, they won't necessarily use that information if they don't see how it will help them. Or they won't necessarily use that information if they do see where using the information will lead to trouble—like when it will be used against them.

This last point is probably the most common reason I have observed why people don't like to provide estimates related to the work they conduct. Too often when software practitioners are asked for an "estimate" whatever they say is then used as a "firm commitment".

Furthermore, too often these "estimates" fail to consider all the related activities that need to be done. And so the common scenario that plays out is one that inevitably leads to bad feelings with practitioners being "beaten up" for missing their so called "commitments," –which in their minds they never really committed to anyway. So why bother?

Upside down coaching tip #15: The value of estimating– beyond knowing when you will be done

To understand why you might want to bother let's take a look at estimating from a different and possibly upside down perspective.

Jack is a tester at NORO. When I asked Jack how long it takes him to run certain test cases, he responded word for word with the phrase,

"I don't have a clue."

And I replied to Jack,

"Ok. I understand you don't have a clue, but just think about the steps you have to go through for each test."

As Jack started to think about it we got into a conversation about his approach to testing. I kept the conversation going with the following question and related thought,

"Jack, do you think ahead of time about all the tests you are planning to run on a given day? By thinking ahead of time about your full day plan, then maybe you could group related tests and save set up time."

Jack replied,

"Yes. That's a good idea. I do try to do that. But sometimes I get into a test and realize I don't know exactly what I should be looking for. Then I need to abort the test until I can get back to the developer to get more information about the change that was made."

I responded,

"If you planned all the tests ahead of time and thought about what you should look for to indicate pass/fail, then you would be able to make sure you had all the information you needed before you wasted the time setting up the test in the first place."

As we talked about how Jack conducts his testing I realized why he was not doing better planning by thinking through his testing scenarios ahead of time. He told me that in the previous company where he worked they had rigorous step by step written test procedures. When he came to NORO he learned that this was a smaller more agile company that was trying to get away from the heavy-weight slow moving bureaucratic processes and that reminded him of what he had been used to at his previous company. So Jack just assumed this meant that writing down his testing scenarios and thinking about them ahead of time was viewed at NORO as an inefficient thing to do.

I explained to Jack that planning his tests ahead of time didn't mean he would be inefficient in the way he worked. I explained that if he did it right, the result would be quite the opposite.

Before this discussion Jack didn't seem to realize that he had any options other than no plan or detailed step by step test procedures.

I explained to Jack how many efficient companies use written test procedures that assume the tester has a level of knowledge of the system so the tester doesn't need to be given detailed step by step procedures. I went on to point out that one value of written– but not detailed step by step– procedures was that they could still provide clear test setup requirements, and essential information related to pass/fail indications. I explained to Jack how this could save him time by eliminating many of his aborted tests.

I sensed that Jack was starting to understand. I then said,

"So Jack, I believe that you are starting to see the value of planning the tests you run ahead of time and the value of written test procedures, but do you also now see the value of estimating how long your testing activities will take?"

Jack replied,

"If I don't write down every step then I still won't know exactly how long it will take me."

I replied,

"Jack, why do you think an estimate needs to be exact? Do you see any other value in creating an estimate?"

At this point Jack had a very confused look on his face and I don't think he had a clue what I was getting at. So let me now explain it more directly.

To estimate effort you need to know what you have to do and be able to make some kind of judgement about the time it will take. By breaking the "what you have to do" down into a number of steps or activities and then estimating the effort involved to complete each piece you are more likely to have a reasonably accurate overall estimate.

However, experience has shown that breaking work down beyond a level at which you understand the work usually results in wasted effort and not a more accurate or useful estimate. Breaking the work down beyond what we know is a common past problem that has led many organizations to abandon the practice of detailed planning. This is unfortunate, because the root of the problem isn't that detailed planning is a waste of time. Rather planning in detail in areas where you don't have a clue what you are really going to do is a waste of time. This brings us back to the tip I shared in the previous story on how to break work down without wasting your time. If you don't recall it, or you skipped it, I suggest you return and read tip #14 now.

What I want the reader to understand about this story is that there is a very good reason to create estimates beyond trying to get an exact number indicating how long a task or activity will take—which, by the way, you will never get anyway.

By getting people to think about their work and how long each piece takes, it also helps them think about other ways they might do their job. This naturally leads them to think about how they might improve the way they work which ultimately leads to more consistent performance, as well as a credible plan.

It has also been my experience that once people start estimating it can be an eye-opening experience. This is because many of us tend to think that certain common activities we do each day take considerably less (or more) time than what they actually take.

When we start to pay more conscious attention to the activities we perform each day in doing our job, and think about how long we spend doing each, it causes us to naturally reflect on how we can continually improve our way of working.

 # Upside Down Principle Twenty-Two:

 Traditional thinking: We need to estimate so we will know exactly when we will be done.

Clarifying thought: No matter how good your processes or your people are, you can never know exactly when you will be done—but this fact is never a good reason not to estimate.

Summary Upside Down Principle 22

<u>Principle Twenty-Two</u>: *We need to estimate so we will know exactly when we will be done*

<u>Extended clarifying thought</u>: An estimate is just that. No matter how good our processes or our people are we can never know exactly when we will be done. But estimating has another value besides giving us an idea when we will be done. It helps us achieve the following two checklists:

· *The team continually tunes their use of the practices and tools*

· *A credible plan is in place*

Story Seven: Upside Down Ideas on Defects and Requirements

Who would disagree with the idea that it is better to find and fix defects early than late? This is what many of us were taught and few would disagree because most of us were taught that the later you find defects in a project the more costly they are to fix. However, this isn't always true.

Upside down coaching tip #16: When is it really more costly to detect defects, and when should you fix them?

Defects are only more costly to fix later in the lifecycle if they were inserted early and you decide you really need to fix them. Another way to think about this seemingly upside down idea is that when we were taught the fundamentals of finding and fixing defects early many of us were thinking "early" from the perspective of a waterfall life cycle, and we were thinking that any defect certainly needs to be fixed.

There are two distinct points I want to make in this section. One about finding defects, the other about fixing them.

First, we have learned over the last 10 to 15 years that it is often better to break a large project into smaller and shorter projects and use an iterative lifecycle. You can even think of each sprint in an agile project as its own project. When you think this way you realize that finding defects late from your overall project perspective can actually be finding them "early" when you think about the defects you are finding early in late sprints.

Second, it is also worth pointing out something we discussed earlier in story three related to decisions to fix defects. That is, just because you have found a defect doesn't necessarily mean you should fix it.

As I pointed out in story three (specifically when we discussed the last of our six categories of defects), developers should always ask a few questions before proceeding to fix a defect.

A fundamental many of us were taught is that the goal should always be "defect-free" software. However, we have learned this is not always the best approach. We have learned that while "defect-free" software sounds great in theory, in practice it never happens. And before fixing any defect, developers should be asking questions such as,

"What are the risks of unintended consequences (e.g. inserting new and potentially more serious defects), if I make this change?"

And

"Just how critical is this defect?"

And

"Are there workarounds to this defect that users can live with that will help us avoid potentially more serious defects?"

Depending on the situation, some defects are better never fixed. I realize this sounds completely upside down from what many of us were taught.

Upside Down Principle Twenty-Three:

 Traditional thinking: It is always better to find and fix defects early.

 Clarifying thought: It is better to find defects close in time to when you insert them—- better yet, find them just before you insert them.

Upside down coaching tip #17: When is the best time to gather requirements?

Let me now share another fundamental many of us were taught that may be upside down.

Is it really always better to gather all your requirements early, even if you can?

At NORO when they had a customer who wanted some new functionality they decided to show that customer the simplest possible solution. NORO did this even though their developers believed what was needed was far more complicated and would take years to build. The traditional thinking has been to push your customer to tell you all the requirements early, but NORO took a different approach.

The idea NORO had was not to ask their customer for all their requirements early. Rather they decided to show the customer the simplest possible solution they could imagine that had any chance of solving the customer's problem. Sometimes when you show someone a solution that is different than what they were thinking, they realize they don't need all the things they thought they needed to solve their problem.

Upside Down Principle Twenty-Four:

 Traditional thinking: Understand all your requirements before you design.

 Clarifying thought: Show your customer the simplest possible solution to their problem before asking them for more requirements.

The other side of the "delaying requirements" argument

It could, of course, be argued that by taking the "delaying requirements" approach just discussed we may be deferring defects until late in the project. However, in fact, we aren't increasing the cost of finding these defects because we haven't inserted them yet.

Finding defects early isn't really the main goal. The real goal is to figure out the simplest thing that could possibly work. A simpler solution reduces the chances of many defects ever happening. In other words, the less software we develop the fewer chances for defect injection. I realize this, again, may sound completely upside down.

Upside down coaching tip #18: Reaffirming the best time to find defects

Note: I want to reaffirm in this tip one key point already made in this story.

What is really important isn't finding defects early, but finding them close in time to when you insert them. Ultimately we want to find them just before we insert them. Or stated differently – we never want to make them in the first place.

Summary Upside Down Principles 23, 24

Principle Twenty-Three: *It is always better to find and fix defects early*

Extended clarifying thought: It is better to find defects close in time to when you insert them. Better yet, find them just before you insert them.

Principle Twenty-Four: *Understand all your requirements before you design*

Extended clarifying thought: Show your customer the simplest possible solution to their problem before you ask them for more requirements. Then work with your customer to understand the most critical requirements that are missing. Then fix just those issues and show them what you have before you ask them for more requirements.

If you don't quite get the point, the old thinking of "understand all your requirements before you design" (which is still a good fundamental) was upside down in the sense that it was interpreted as "ask your customer for all their requirements before you do any work".

Unfortunately this led many organizations into product visions that were far more complicated than what was needed. This often occurred because of a failure in communication early with regard to the real need that was driving the requirements.

A root cause of this failure was often the fact that the customer actually didn't know their requirements, and we weren't doing enough communicating with them concerning what they actually needed. Seeing a demonstration of a product in operation is one way that has been proven to cut through many of these costly miscommunications.

Story Eight: Upside Down Ideas at Facebook

In 2015 I travelled to South Africa for the first time in my life when I was invited to speak at the Agile Africa Conference in Johannesburg. One of my favorite memories from this trip was getting to personally meet and listen to Kent Beck speak. I had known of Kent's work with Extreme Programming and Test-Driven Development, but what I found most interesting on this trip was listening to Kent in his keynote address [10] where he talked about the way work gets done at Facebook.

Upside down policies at Facebook

In his keynote Kent didn't talk at all about the software development practices used at Facebook. Rather he focused on what he called policies – or what many of us might call principles. As I listened to Kent speak what struck me was how much you could learn about the way developers actually worked at Facebook just from hearing these policies which Kent indicated came directly from Mark Zuckenberg's vision. One of those policies Kent referred to as "personal ownership." As an example of personal ownership at Facebook, Kent said that a sign on the back of his door reads:

"Nothing at Facebook is somebody else's problem."

In describing what this policy meant Kent talked about what he called "dependency breakers". He said:

"People learn quickly at Facebook never to go into a meeting and say they can't get something done because they are waiting on someone else to finish a certain task."

Kent also explained how developers implement this policy by emphasizing that everyone at Facebook quickly learns to focus on eliminating dependencies.

It sounded completely upside down from everything I was taught. For example, if you are dependent on someone else finishing a task to complete your task, you either stop what you are doing and do something else, or you build something to replace that dependency. That is how you break dependencies at Facebook, and that is what everyone is expected to do.

At Facebook no one ever builds a big complicated schedule with extensive dependencies built in showing all kinds of things that individuals in the organization can't control. This sounds completely upside down because many of us were taught to identify all dependencies and put them on a schedule so they can become a focus for management attention.

⚷ Upside Down Principle Twenty-Five:

 <u>Traditional thinking</u>: Ensure your schedule identifies all major dependencies.

 <u>Clarifying thought</u>: Rather than focusing on identifying dependencies, focus on eliminating them.

It may sound upside down, but...

The crazy part is that at Facebook this upside down idea works! They get stuff done and fast. People deploy software fast. For example, within two weeks of being hired at Facebook you are expected to be affecting the Facebook product that is released and being used by people around the world.

Change approvals and software breakage at Facebook

Now, given these policies, wouldn't you think that there would be some serious approval processes in place to make sure inexperienced developers weren't breaking the released software?

Well, at Facebook that doesn't happen. In fact, at Facebook there aren't a lot of meetings where stuff gets approved before it goes into a release. The way they deal with problems is quite different from most organizations. If someone breaks something at Facebook, someone will fix it. That's just the way they work. It goes back to the personal ownership policy. And they don't have a problem with people blaming others for breakage. In fact, if you like to blame someone else for a problem, Kent said you probably won't be working at Facebook very long.

Now, some might quickly object that these policies could never work for mission critical software. And if it works at Facebook it is only because it's a social media application and no one is going to die if part of Facebook is broken for a few hours.

While this may be true, the point is that these policies work given appropriate situations. And it has been my experience that even in large mission critical project environments there are situations where what might otherwise be a completely inappropriate practice, presents the perfect answer.

A quick example that comes to mind is while a "zero-defect" policy may be appropriate for mission critical embedded flight control software, when it comes to ground station support software on the same project, the situation may be different. For example, the customer for support software may be able to live with certain defects as long as they have acceptable work-arounds.

Listening to Kent explain the way people work at Facebook caused me to stop and think about how principles (or policies) relate to practices and how they affect the way work gets done.

The power of principles in guiding developers

As an example, when I was involved in the development of the Essence framework I recall not fully appreciating some of the checklists in the first few states of the Way of Working Alpha.

The first state is *"Principles Established"* and two of the checklists follow:

· *The principles and constraints are committed to by the team*

· *The principles and constraints are agreed to by the stake-holders*

What I didn't fully understand when we were creating these states and checklists was the power of principles in guiding a developer's decisions.

Listening to Kent Beck helped me to see the power of principles, not just at Facebook, but in any situation, and it helped me understand how principles can help teams with their practices. Scott Ambler also told me that with Disciplined

Agile Delivery (DAD) [11] they emphasize principles because people might actually read them and understand them. Let me now share an example.

At NORO over the first six sprints as I worked with the team to evolve their practices a few principles emerged.

Principle One:

We won't send the customer a product that has not been adequately tested.

Clarifying Note:

We may send the customer a product with some known defects, but if we do we will be open about those defects in our release notes which will include the plan to solve them, along with recommended workarounds.

Principle Two:

We expect constant communication between developers and testers

Clarifying Note:

We always expect our testers to be clear on what they have to do to test any software a developer has worked on. This may be achieved through direct communication between tester and developer or by the developer adding notes to the ticket, or a combination of both.

Principle Three:

We always conduct regression testing prior to any release, including quick patch releases

Clarifying Note:

Our product is used in many different configurations by different customers and so we know we can't possibly test all configurations for each release. Therefore we always give thought to the types of changes we are making in each release and we conduct "focused regression testing" covering the most likely problem areas based on past experience.

Observation on principles and practices

My observations about these principles (or policies) is not meant to imply that we don't still need good processes and best practices. Best practices will always be needed. However, when teams understand the specific weaknesses that hold back their performance and when they discover for themselves what they need to do to get better, strong cultures based on committed principles emerge that lead to the consistent higher predictable performance we all seek.

Upside Down Principle Twenty-Six:

 Traditional thinking: To work effectively all your team members need to be fully trained in all your organizational practices.

 Clarifying thought: Understanding agreed to and committed principles can often help teams achieve the real intent of organizational practices better than the practices themselves.

Summary Upside Down Principles 25, 26

Principle Twenty-Five: *Ensure your schedule identifies all major dependencies*

Extended clarifying thought: Rather than focusing on identifying dependencies, focus on eliminating them.

Principle Twenty-Six: *To work effectively all your team members need to be fully trained in all your organizational practices*

Extended clarifying thought: Understanding agreed to and committed principles can often help teams achieve the real intent of organizational practices better than the practices themselves.

PART II

Essence

In this part of the book you will find

- motivation and introduction to Essence
- an explanation of the relationship between the stories in Part I and Essence
- an explanation of the relationship between each principle in Part I and Essence
- an example of an essentialized practice from one of my stories in Part I
- a summary of the 26 upside down principles in an essentialized form

I also explain through the example of an essentialized practice (which includes a brief introduction to the Essence language) how anyone can use the Essence language to capture the questions that should be asked– in a checklist form– and the activities recommended to be conducted, such as those I share in Part I of this book. But before we get into a discussion of Essence, let me motivate why you should care about this framework by providing a little background.

Motivation for Essence

Essence is based on the Software Engineering Method and Theory (SEMAT) initiative [12] which was initiated at the end of 2009 envisioned by Ivar Jacobson, and two advisors Bertrand Meyer and Richard Soley. There are many people from around the world, including industry, academia and research, who worked as volunteers leading to the Essence Object Management Group (OMG) standard. While Essence has only been an OMG standard since 2014, its roots can be traced back to 2005 when Ivar Jacobson International (IJI) redesigned the Rational Unified Process (RUP) and presented this as ESSUP (the Essential Unified Process).

One of the prime motivators behind SEMAT is stated on the SEMAT web site [12] :

"There are millions of software engineers on the planet in countless programs, projects and teams; the millions of lines of software that run the world are testament to their talents. However, as a community we still find it difficult to share our best practices, truly empower our teams, seamlessly integrate software engineering with other engineering disciplines and into our businesses, and maintain the health of our endeavors avoiding embarrassing and unnecessary catastrophic failures.

The industry's habit of constantly switching between no method and the latest "one true way" (an affliction that sadly is even affecting the agile community) is not the way forward."

The SEMAT community is not alone in observing this trend. Capers Jones, who has been collecting data on software quality, risks and best practices for many years told me that software engineering has created more variations of software methods than any other engineering discipline in human history.

What makes this situation a serious problem

This situation, in itself, might not present a serious problem, if we had a reasonably efficient way to:

- compare these varying methods, identifying the unique discriminating value of each
- extract specific unique discriminating pieces of a method to use on a given endeavor together with whatever an organization is already doing

Unfortunately, this is not the case today. Most of these methods come hopelessly entangled with basic non-discriminating information– which may well be useful for beginners– but provides little, if any, added value to software professionals who have been working in industry for a few years or more.

What does this problem have to do with the stories in Part I of this book and Essence?

There is a common trait shared by all my stories in Part I of this book where we were able to rapidly provide measurable performance improvement. I, as a coach, did not attempt to change what was working well in my client organizations. I did not try to convince my clients NORO and NANO to embrace an entirely new method. But rather, in each case, I drilled down by asking a series of questions to get as close as possible to the real root cause of the problem being faced.

Then we put small "micro-surgical-like" changes in place that were intended to carefully address specific issues identified, while not disturbing the fundamental foundation within the organization that was already in place and working well. This leads us to Essence.

The simple idea that rests at the heart of Essence

This simple idea of separating the core fundamentals from specific practices, techniques, tips and patterns that focus on solving specific challenges within an organization rests at the heart of what Essence is about.

It is about providing a framework that has a "common ground" that has been proven to exist on all successful software engineering efforts. It is about agreeing on how to talk about this common ground in a way that we don't need to relearn every time a software professional comes up with a potentially new and better idea. It is about agreeing on a simple way to express small changes to our way of working so our teams can improve and keep improving without stepping back each time relearning again and again what we all know to be true.

What follows in this part of the book

In the following section I provide a brief introduction to Essence. I also share a simple example of a practice I developed for one of my clients, which also shows how to highlight the unique value of a practice. This approach allows organizations to train their new developers in what is unique and discriminating about their approach without needing to retrain them in fundamentals they learned in school, and don't need to constantly relearn again and again. This, of course, does not mean that people don't at times need refresher training, or reminders, in the basics. But separating the basics can make this kind of training more efficient as well.

What is Essence?

I often refer to Essence as a "thinking framework" developed specifically to help software practitioners "think-through" the common issues they face each day on the job leading to better decisions. But, in fact, it is more than just a "thinking framework." It is a framework that can be applied with whatever practices, method and tools a team is already using. It includes a set of checklists applicable to all software engineering endeavors. These checklists are part of the "common ground" part of Essence that is relevant to all successful software engineering efforts.

It is the checklists that give the framework its "thinking-aid" characteristics. Essence also includes a simple language that allows practitioners and organizations to express specific practices as separate and distinct extensions to the common ground. I will talk more about the language in a moment, but first let me say a little more about the checklists.

When you read the Essence checklists included in this part of the book your first reaction may be that they are obvious and therefore should require little attention. But I suggest you think about them again in the context of the stories I provide in Part I of this book. I believe, based on my many years of working with software development teams, that when you consider these checklists thoughtfully in the context of real stories their power becomes evident.

As a simple example– but one that I hope strikes home with you when you read my stories– many essential, but seemingly obvious, software engineering fundamentals often missed by development teams are done so because conscious activity and effort is still required to achieve them. And, far too often, the activity that is needed isn't what many of us have believed for many years based on what we were taught.

This is a primary point of my stories in Part I of this book. If this point isn't clear to you right now, please

return and review Story Two where I provide four specific examples of why teams vary in their activities to achieve performance goals.

I will shortly explain further how Essence can help with this dilemma when I get back in the next section discussing the Essence language. But first, let me say more about the essential fundamentals that Essence provides and how those fundamentals relate to the 26 upside down principles discusssed in Part I of this book.

The Essence framework uses the term "alpha" to identify the essential things we work with that exist on all software engineering endeavors. There are seven alphas in the Essence framework and their names should be familiar to everyone. This is because the names were chosen intentionally to fit naturally with what we have learned is essential to all successful software development efforts. Figure Part II-1 identifies the seven essential alphas and shows how the 26 upside down principles discussed in Part I of this book relate to those essential items.

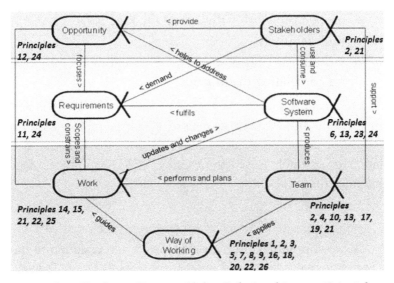

Figure Part II-1 Seven Essence Alphas Relationship to 26 Principles

Now I want to get back to the Essence language and explain the value it can bring beyond the essential fundamentals.

A Simple Example Illustrating "Essentializing" a Practice Using the Essence Language

"Essentializing" a practice means capturing the "essence" of the practice using the Essence language. Let me now explain this process, along with the value it can bring, through a simple example from Part I of this book. If you recall from Story One and Story Two, I explained how I helped NORO by coaching them through their first few sprints and then I produced "lite" documentation for nine practices that NORO was using. Each practice was documented using a simple 3 page template that included

- a brief description of the purpose of the practice
- activities to conduct during the practice
- products to work with during the practice
- roles required
- 3 checklists (for preparing, for executing the practice, for completing the practice)

In creating these practices I used a subset of the Essence graphical language. Figure Part II-2 shows the four Essence language symbols I used to describe NORO's practices. This includes the symbol for

- activities to conduct when executing the practice
- work products used, or modified when conducting the practice
- competencies required to conduct the practice
- patterns used to help when conducting the practice

For the purposes of this illustration I have added a fifth symbol to represent the related Essence alpha. **Identifying the related alpha(s) is critical when "essentializing" a practice because it keeps the "common ground" reference visible helping people quickly see potential gaps, as well as where** unique discriminators of a practice can help– which are both key reasons for essentializing.

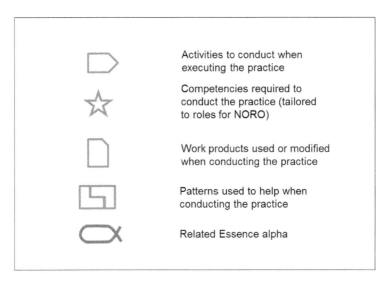

Figure Part II-2 Essence Language Symbols Used for NORO's Practices

You can think of a pattern as anything (such as a technique) that can help teams conduct a practice more effectively. Defining a role with a list of responsibilities is one way that patterns can be used in the Essence language. Although roles are different from competencies, at NORO the team decided to use the competency symbol to identify key roles in their tailored Scrum approach.

A simple example that is similar to what I used to help NORO improve their risk management approach is a risk identification and analysis practice. Figure Part II-3 shows an overview of this practice which includes

- a purpose statement
- things to do (activities)

- things to work with (work products)
- roles required to conduct the practice
- a pattern used to help conduct the practice

Title: NORO Risk Identification and Analysis Practice

Purpose: Use this practice to stimulate risk discussions, assess risk significance, and agree on appropriate risk mitigation activities to be performed this sprint.

It includes basic instructions on the performance of the risk practice, a simple technique to measure risk significance, and a simple technique to generate risk discussion.

Things to do:	Things to work with:
• Conduct risk assessment	• Risk List

Roles required:	Pattern
• Product Owner	• Facilitate risk discussion using Essence framework
• Scrum Master	
• All Developers	

Figure Part II-3 NORO Risk Practice-1

Figure Part II-4 shows key information related to the activity of conducting the practice which includes

- a risk list work product used as an input to the activity
- work products modified or produced by conducting the activity
- how to conduct the activity
- Essence alpha the practice is related to

Conduct Risk Identification and Analysis Activity

On Entry

Current risk list

How to conduct activity:

Facilitated by Scrum Master as part of Sprint Planning where the team:
- Brainstorms potential risks
- Assesses significance of each risk candidate
- Agrees on risks to be mitigated this sprint
- Agrees on activity to mitigate the risk
- Assigns personnel to conduct activity and report on risk status

Roles Required

All Developers
Scrum Master
Product Owner

On Exit
Updated risk list
Agreed activities to mitigate risks
Risk ownership assigned personnel

Way of Working

Figure Part II-4 NORO Risk Practice-2

Figure Part II-5 shows

- checklists used at NORO to help the team prepare to conduct the practice
- checklist to help the team conduct the practice
- checklist to help with completion of practice (e.g. are we done?)
- who is responsible for each checklist (e.g. ScrumMaster for preparing)

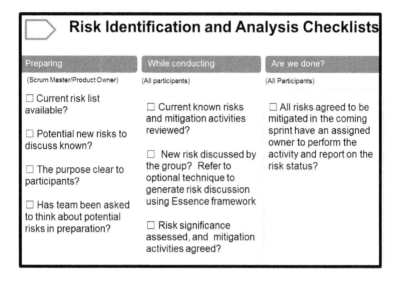

Risk Identification and Analysis Checklists

Preparing	While conducting	Are we done?
(Scrum Master/Product Owner)	(All participants)	(All Participants)
☐ Current risk list available?	☐ Current known risks and mitigation activities reviewed?	☐ All risks agreed to be mitigated in the coming sprint have an assigned owner to perform the activity and report on the risk status?
☐ Potential new risks to discuss known?	☐ New risk discussed by the group? Refer to optional technique to generate risk discussion using Essence framework	
☐ The purpose clear to participants?		
☐ Has team been asked to think about potential risks in preparation?	☐ Risk significance assessed, and mitigation activities agreed?	

Figure Part II-5 NORO Risk Practice-3

Figure Part II-6 shows what we called the "Facilitate risk discussion using the Essence framework" pattern. This pattern was used to help stimulate risk discussions– as discussed in Story One– concerning the risk raised by the Scrum Master related to the team continually being interrupted by stakeholders who had not been properly trained in the new process.

⌐ Facilitate Risk Discussion Using Essence Framework

Pattern Description: A simple technique that a team can use to quickly generate risk discussion during sprint planning

Equipment: Whiteboard or flip chart; Sticky notes

Basic instructions:
1. Scrum Master or Product Owner leads group through 7 Alphas, using checklists to stimulate discussion of possible risks
2. Scrum Master generates discussion by asking: do we have any risks in this area?
3. Anyone can use a sticky note to capture a risk for potential discussion
4. Scrum Master captures results

Alternatively, the Scrum Master or the Product Owner could use the Essence Alphas and checklists prior to the sprint planning session to conduct this activity alone or with a smaller group, and then use the results to expedite and stimulate the risk discussion with the full group during sprint planning.

Figure Part II-6 NORO Risk Practice-4

For more information on Essence refer to [1, 2, 3, 4].

So why should you care about "Essentializing" practices?

After looking at the essentialized risk identification and analysis practice described above that I developed for NORO, you might be wondering why you should care about essentializing practices. You may also be wondering how this practice is any different from what you are doing in your organization today. Let me give you a simple scenario to help explain the value.

When I first started working with NORO (refer to Part I, Story Two) I quickly discovered that they needed significant help with risk management. This was because their poor risk management approach was causing real pain in their organization. We needed to focus on risk identification and analysis to help them rapidly solve real challenges that were hurting their performance. The checklists in this practice were developed to address specific weaknesses observed at NORO.

At NANO their highest priority problems were different. As an example (refer to Story Three), at NANO we focused on how to help the team conduct better peer reviews to reduce escaping defects. This led to an improved peer review process with checklists developed specifically to remind the NORO team members of common trouble spots in their product and the names of experts at NORO they could call for help when needed.

The simple point that I hope you are getting from these examples is that the most effective and practical path to real performance improvement occurs continually and most often in small steps focused on current real pain points observed in your specific organization, or specific endeavor. But to make the most valuable small steps you need a framework that helps you locate your most important gaps that are hurting your organization, or your current endeavor, today.

What too many organizations miss today

When you essentialize, you also modularize and streamline your practices which means you are organizing and structuring your practices in a way that supports continual improvments in small steps. Essentialization supports your decisions related to where to place emphasis in your practices, such as on **activities to conduct, how much** of those activities should be conducted, and **when** those activities are best conducted.

As a simple example of the value essentialization can bring, when I help organizations that have practices that were not put together using a common ground reference I often find steps in practices that appear to having nothing to do with the intended purpose of the practice. This is just one value that a common ground reference can bring to your practices. It first helps you break up your practices into small pieces, each with a clear purpose and clear relationship to one or more essentials. This step in turn allows you to see gaps more clearly.

And, most importantly– and what too many organizations miss today– it helps if you focus each improvement step on discriminating value that addresses clear pain points that are impacting your team's performance today.

Viewing Principles as Essentialized "Mini-Practices"

Let me start this section with some motivation for emphasizing principles.

A practice in the Essence language is defined as:

"a repeatable approach to doing something with a specific objective in mind."

In the clarifying thought for upside down principle twenty-six it is pointed out that:

"Understanding agreed to and committed principles can often help teams achieve the real intent of organizational practices better than the practices themselves."

A good example of this clarifying thought is provided in Story Eight where we explained how principles (or policies) provide great insight into how work gets done at Facebook. As further evidence supporting the value of principles, I mentioned in that story that Scott Ambler told me with DAD they emphasize principles because people might actually read them and understand them.

Taking this thought a bit further one can view principles as "mini-practices." From an Essence perspective the **"extended clarifying thoughts"** provided in the summary sections for each principle at the end of each story in Part I (and provided later in this part of the book) can be viewed as **"clarifying activities"** to help effectively apply the principle (or the "mini-practice").

In the remainder of this section a view of the 26 upside down principles as essentialized "mini-practices" is provided. The relationship of each principle to Essence alphas, and checklists is included. References back to the relevant stories in Part I are also provided.

When Essence checklists relevant to a principle in the book are identified, the Essence alpha they are a part of is also identified. The format used to identify the alpha associated with each checklist item is: <u>AlphaName</u>: Checklist item.

As you review each upside down principle and related Essence checklists, I suggest you also review the relevant stories from Part I focusing on the questions I asked and the activities I suggested my clients conduct to help them solve their challenges and improve their performance.

A suggested exercise

As an exercise you could also use the previously provided example of an essentialized practice (risk identification and analysis practice) as a template to create simple practices that capture appropriate variations of my questions– in the suggested checklist form– and recommended activities that fit with your own situation. These simple practice aids can then be used to help guide your teams when their coach is not available.

Upside Down Principle One:

 Traditional thinking: Plan and define your process before you use your process.

Extended clarifying thought/ Clarifying activities:

Conduct just enough planning and definition for your team to move forward using the key processes needed to get started so they can prove them out, and refine them with improvements that work best for their situation.

✔ Essence Checklists Relevant to Principle:

- Way of Working: Enough practices for work to start are agreed to by the team

Essence Checklist Clarifying Note: A team doesn't need all their practices defined at the start of their endeavor, nor do they need all the details of their practices to start making useful progress and learning more about how to improve their performance.

Reference Story: Introduction; "Do we really need to define our processes?"

Upside Down Principle Two:

 Traditional thinking: Focus your improvement efforts on industry "best practices".

Extended   clarifying   thought/   Clarifying activities:

While industry best practices and lessons are useful, they cannot replace listening to your practitioners, understanding their needs and understanding the specific needs and constraints of your stakeholders, environment and your product.

✔ Essence Checklists Relevant to Principle:

- Team: Any constraints on where and how the work is carried out are defined
- Stakeholders: The collaboration approach among the stakeholder representatives has been agreed
- Way of Working: Any practice and tool constraints are known

Essence Checklists Clarifying Note: Too often critical constraints are not adequately considered when preparing and agreeing to how the team will operate. As an example, someone needs to take on the responsibility to ensure key stakeholders agree to their responsibilities and how they will carry them out working collaboratively with the team. A specific example of this can be seen in many Scrum teams that fail because they fail to get their key stakeholders to agree to attend periodic sprint reviews and provide feedback.

Reference Story: Introduction; Specfically "Are industry "best practices" best for you?"

Upside Down Principle Three:

 Traditional thinking: You need to establish measures first to be sure any process changes lead to real performance improvement.

Extended clarifying thought/ Clarifying activities:

In general measuring is important to be sure you aren't fooling yourself, but sometimes it's easier to just fix the problem when everyone agrees and you know how to fix it.

✔ Essence Checklists Relevant to Principle:

- Way of Working: The practices and tools are being used by the whole team to perform their work

Essence Checklist Clarifying Note: The phrase "whole team" needs to be interpreted by each team given their own context. Sometimes the view of your team needs to be extended beyond those actively involved every day in carrying out the work to include stakeholders who can affect the team's way of working, as we saw in Story One at NORO.

<u>Reference Story:</u> Story One; Refer to this story for a good example of how a team can rapidly fix a problem without measuring first, when everyone agrees on what the problem is, and they know how to fix it.

Upside Down Principle Four:

 Traditional thinking: Showing management hard data related to a problem is the best way to get them to support a needed process change.

 Extended clarifying thought/ Clarifying activities:

Showing management hard data related to a problem, along with hard data that demonstrates a real solution that has been proven to work is the best way to get them to support a needed process change. Often, in cases where the problem relates to a team being constantly interrupted, solutions to root causes are found in helping team members understand the full extent of their responsibilities.

✔ Essence Checklists Relevant to Principle:

- Team: Every team member understands how the team is organized and what their individual role is
- Team: All team members understand how to perform their work

<u>Essence Checklist Clarifying Note:</u> A role includes a set of responsibilities. As we saw in the Story One at NORO, key to solving the problem of the team constantly being interrupted was getting all team members to understand the product owner role and what it meant to how they performed their work.

<u>Reference Story:</u> Story One

Upside Down Principle Five:

 Traditional thinking: If you use the CMMI framework you need to focus on the level 2 process areas before attacking level 3 (refer to staged implementation of CMMI).

Extended   clarifying   thought/   Clarifying activities:

The CMMI framework is a model. No model reflects real situations perfectly. Use it as a guide, not a set of dictated, ordered processes.

✔ Essence Checklists Relevant to Principle:

- Way of Working: The gaps that exist between the practices and tools that are needed and the practices and tools that are available have been analyzed and understood

Essence Checklist Clarifying Note: Assessing practice (or process) gaps should generate discussion among team members leading to agreement on which gaps are most important to address now, as we saw at NORO in Story Two. Depending on your specific situation the most important gaps to fill first can vary greatly.

Reference Story: Story Two

Upside Down Principle Six:

<u>Traditional thinking</u>: You should have a well-defined repeatable test process, and always test completely with a goal of zero defects before you release.

<u>Extended   clarifying   thought/   Clarifying</u> <u>activities</u>:

Often in today's fast-paced competitive world organizations don't have enough time to test everything completely before each release. One practical and proven approach is to test just the pieces your team has focused on during this release, and any prior released functionality to ensure it still works. Then aggressively focus on letting everyone know the limitations of what is in the current release. This means being open and honest with what this release does and does not do, and what will be coming in future releases.

✔ Essence Checklists Relevant to Principle:

- <u>Software System</u>: Defect levels are acceptable to the stakeholders

<u>Essence Checklist Clarifying Note</u>: On most projects there is limited test time so you need to focus that time on the area

most critical to the needs of your customer and the agreed to scope of the current released product. We don't necessarily need a "defect-free" product, but we do need a product where the "defect levels are acceptable to the stakeholders." As an example, this can mean where defects do exist acceptable work-arounds have been defined and have been communicated to the users, as we saw in Story Two at NORO.

Reference Story: Story Two

Upside Down Principle Seven:

 Traditional thinking: You have to prove out your processes on a pilot project before using them for real.

Extended   clarifying   thought/   Clarifying activities:

You have to prove out your processes on a project that reflects the real conditions your practitioners most often face each day.

✔ Essence Checklists Relevant to Principle:

- Way of Working: The team continually tunes their use of the practices and tools

Essence Checklist Clarifying Note: Refer back to Story Two, if you don't recall why the best projects to tune the use of the practices and tools are projects involving real customers with real project deliverables and deadlines.

Reference Story: Story Two

Upside Down Principle Eight:

 Traditional thinking: You need to hold your processes stable during a project to avoid risk.

Extended clarifying thought/ Clarifying activities:

Allowing your team to "continually tune their use of the practices and tools" as they learn, and doing so in small steps that can be reviewed and revised as necessary in short iterations– while it may seem upside down from what we have been taught– it is actually the best way to achieve real and sustainable repeatable results. And the real goal is repeatable results, not a repeatable controlled stable process.

It is also worth emphasizing here that such tuning needs to be done within a structure that provides clear limits to acceptable tuning. Otherwise we risk chaos.

✔ Essence Checklists Relevant to Principle:

- Way of Working: Predictable progress is being made by the team

<u>Essence Checklist Clarifying Note:</u> Until a process is proven in a real project environment there is high risk it is not the best process to be using, and therefore is likely to hinder rather than help progress.

<u>Reference Story:</u> Story Two

Upside Down Principle Nine:

 Traditional thinking: You have to produce your process documentation before your teams use your processes on real projects.

👍 Extended clarifying thought/ Clarifying activities:

Teams do need to know how to use key practices and tools selected for your project. But key practices and tools often provide just a starting point for what practitioners need to know to perform well on most projects. As an example, they need checklists with reminders, and you can't produce the most useful checklists at the start of the project because many of the most useful checklists reflect what the team learns while performing on a real project.

✔ Essence Checklists Relevant to Principle:

- Way of Working: [Add your own checklists as you learn and improve..]

Essence Checklist Clarifying Note:

For those who are using Essence, teams are encouraged to add their own checklists to the Essence checklists as they learn and improve.

Refer to Story Two; "Why waiting to document isn't upside down", where I explain how we used the Essence checklists to get started, but also created additional checklists based on the team's own experiences.

Reference Story: Story Two

Upside Down Principle Ten:

 Traditional thinking: Developers need to think-through all potential impacts to ensure their design is complete.

👍 Extended clarifying thought/ Clarifying activities:

Just telling developers to "think-through all potential impacts" is sometimes just not practical. With many complicated legacy systems developers often do not have sufficient product knowledge to understand all potential change impacts. Creating a list of common "trouble spots" and contact experts can help mitigate the risk of software breakage due to unanticipated side-effects of changes.

✔ Essence Checklists Relevant to Principle:

- Team: Team members know each other
- Team: Team members are working as one unit
- Team: The team is focused on the mission

Essence Checklist Clarifying Note:

Team members need to know other team members who are experts in key areas and can help them. Experts need to know that helping teammates in the area of their expertise is part of their responsibilities. And the team needs to agree on the mission so they can predict the effort required from each team member.

Reference Story: Story Three; "We did not think through all the potential impacts"

Upside Down Principle Eleven:

<u>Traditional thinking</u>: If you don't have all the requirements you need, just make the best assumptions.

<u>Extended clarifying thought/ Clarifying activities:</u>

If you don't have all the requirements you need, first talk to a peer or subject matter expert with a little more knowledge to ensure your assumptions are valid. Second, document assumptions in a place that is visible to the testers and anyone else with a need to know.

✔ Essence Checklists Relevant to Principle:

- <u>Requirements</u>: Conflicting requirements are identified and attended to

<u>Essence Checklist Clarifying Note:</u>

When you make assumptions related to requirements, one way of "attending to" those decisions is to document the assumptions and let the testers (as well as your project leader) know about them.

<u>Reference Story:</u> Story Three; "We didn't get all the requirements so we had to make assumptions"

Upside Down Principle Twelve:

 Traditional thinking: Once a requirement/use case has been accepted by the customer the team can be confident that their software works as intended.

Extended clarifying thought/ Clarifying activities:

It is not uncommon, especially on large complicated legacy systems, for certain capabilities not to be used when initially released, but then used by customers in later releases. Therefore teams need to work closely with key stakeholders to understand their needs and vision for each upcoming product release.

Essence Checklists Relevant to Principle:

- Opportunity: The Stakeholders' needs that generate the opportunity have been established
- Opportunity: Any underlying problems and their root causes have been identified

Essence Checklist Clarifying Note:

Stakeholder needs can change from release to release. Therefore someone on the team should be responsible for reviewing the needs with each release. A stakeholder's high priority problems can also change from release to release. Therefore someone on the team should be responsible to review the high priority problems each release.

Reference Story: Story Three; "This was a new use case never used before"

Upside Down Principle Thirteen:

 <u>Traditional thinking</u>: You need to read the system documentation to understand how the software works.

<u>Extended clarifying thought/ Clarifying activities</u>:

Often teams cannot trust system documentation because it isn't kept up to date, but this doesn't alleviate the need for key team members to understand the technical limitations of the system. This need is often best addressed by ensuring team members know other team members who have the critical knowledge they may need. And if the system documentation is not trusted, do something to make it, at least, a little bit better right now.

✔ Essence Checklists Relevant to Principle:

- <u>Team</u>: Team members know each other
- <u>Team</u>: Team members are working as one unit
- <u>Software System</u>: The system is fully documented

Essence Checklist Clarifying Note:

Team members need to know other team members who understand the technical limitations of the system. Team members who understand the technical limitations of the system need to know that sharing their knowledge with other team members is part of their responsibilities.

It is also worth pointing out that the phrase "fully documented" is not meant to imply "heavy-weight" documentation. It means "essential" documentation is available.

Reference Story: Story Three; "Testers don't understand the technical limitations of the system"

Upside Down Principle Fourteen:

 <u>Traditional thinking</u>: If developers are formally trained in programming and unit testing techniques, we can be confident their work will be high quality.

<u>Extended clarifying thought/ Clarifying activities</u>:

While most defects should be caught by developers during low level testing activities, there are many common situations that arise where developers know there is higher likelihood of "escaped" defects. In these cases developers should take the time to communicate associated risks and potential need for additional testing. One proven good practice is to add checklists to remind developers of such common situations and to pay particular attention in these situations to ensure the work is adequately broken down with a clear definition of what "done" means. The more specific the checklists can be the better, such as reminders of past product trouble spots.

✔ Essence Checklists Relevant to Principle:

- <u>Work</u>: The work is being broken down into actionable work items with clear definition of done
- <u>Work</u>: Risks are under control as the impact if they occur and the likelihood of them occurring have been reduced to acceptable levels

<u>Essence Checklist Clarifying Note:</u>

Developers need "clear definition of done" to help them understand how much low level testing is needed. Developers also need to know what options they have to mitigate risk when a ticket they have been assigned to work is not clear with respect to exactly what the problem is.

<u>Reference Story:</u> Story Three; "This was sloppy coding"

Upside Down Principle Fifteen:

 <u>Traditional thinking</u>: Whenever a developer sees a potential problem in the software, a change should be made to address the potential problem.

<u>Extended clarifying thought/ Clarifying activities</u>:

While we want to avoid potential problems, anytime you make a change to the software you add risk of unintended consequences. Therefore, before proceeding with a change, this risk should always be assessed against the significance of the potential problem.

 Essence Checklists Relevant to Principle:

- <u>Work</u>: Re-work is under control

<u>Essence Checklist Clarifying Note:</u>

Developers need to know that whenever they make a change there is risk of unintended software side-effects (e.g. breakage to other software), which can lead to re-work.

<u>Reference Story</u>: Story Three; "Developer decided to make a change because.."

Upside Down Principle Sixteen:

 Traditional thinking: Training your team in a formal classroom setting is the best way to ensure your team will have the skills and competencies they need to produce high quality results.

 Extended clarifying thought/ Clarifying activities:

While formal classroom training focusing on industry best practices can help, on-the-job coaching can often help practitioners more from the perspective of learning how to apply industry best practices in their own project situation.

✔ Essence Checklists Relevant to Principle:

- Way of Working: The whole team is involved in the inspection and adaptation of the way of working

Essence Checklist Clarifying Note:

On-the-job coaching is one proven approach that can help remind practitioners of their responsibility to continually inspect and adapt their way of working.

<u>Reference Stories:</u> Story Three; This story provides multiple examples of the value of on-the-job coaching over formal classroom training

Extending Upside Down Principle Three:

 Traditional thinking: You need to establish measures first to be sure changes lead to real performance improvement.

 Extended   Clarifying   thought/   Clarifying activities:

Sometimes the most practical and meaningful measures can be identified right at the point where you know you have improved your performance.

✔ Essence Checklists Relevant to Principle:

- Way of Working: The team naturally applies the practices without thinking about them

Essence Checklist Clarifying Note:

This checklist is not meant to imply that the team doesn't need to "think". Rather it means they have learned to apply the practices naturally in the common situations they face each day.

<u>Reference Story:</u> Story Three; "An upside down approach to measurement", which provides an example of measuring right at the point where a team knows they have improved performance.

Upside Down Principle Seventeen:

 <u>Traditional thinking</u>: Training people in a classroom setting in roles and responsibilities is the best way to ensure they know their responsibilities and can carry them out.

<u>Extended clarifying thought/ Clarifying activities</u>:

Coaching practitioners in their responsibilities during real project situations can be more effective than classroom training at helping them achieve the competency they need to carry out their responsibilities appropriately each day on the job.

✔ Essence Checklists Relevant to Principle:

- <u>Team</u>: The team members understand their responsibilities and how they align with their competencies

<u>Essence Checklist Clarifying Note:</u>

Team members often read a list of their responsibilities and think they understand them. However, too often they fail to realize that part of the competency they need in carrying out those responsibilities is recognizing the on-the-job situations where those responsibilities come into play. Refer back to my experience coaching Jed at NORO described in Story Four, Tip #1, and to the discussions described in that story on helping team members with their responsibilities.

Reference Story: Story Four; Coaching Tip #1

Upside Down Principle Eighteen:

 Traditional thinking: Training team members in general peer review guidelines is the best way to ensure effective reviews are conducted.

 Extended clarifying thought/ Clarifying activities:

While it is true that general peer review guidelines can be shared and used across diverse products, product-specific checklists are often more effective at helping team members learn to conduct high quality reviews that surface common problems. An example is provided in Story Four where I explain what I learned about how Jed does peer reviews and how it ties to his knowledge of the product architecture.

✔ Essence Checklists Relevant to Principle:

- Way of Working: The whole team is involved in the inspection and adaptation of the way of working

<u>Essence Checklist Clarifying Note:</u>

Sometimes team members don't realize that they are in the best position to inspect and suggest adaptations to improve their way of working. The reason they are in the best position is because they know better than anyone else what is working well, and what isn't working well to help them get their job done. Therefore, all team members need to know that inspection and adaptation of the team's way of working is part of every team member's responsibilities.

If the importance of the previous checklist item is not clear to you, refer back to the multiple examples in Story Two demonstrating how the NORO team adapted their way of working in ways that I, as an external coach, could not possibly have accomplished without the team's significant involvement.

<u>Reference Stories:</u> Story Four; Coaching Tip #3; Story Two; the multiple ways the team adapted their own way of working

Upside Down Principle Nineteen:

 <u>Traditional thinking</u>: Anyone who can code, can peer review code.

<u>Extended clarifying thought/ Clarifying activities</u>:

It takes experience and product-specific knowledge to know where to focus your peer review effort when you have limited time (and we all have limited time).

✔ Essence Checklists Relevant to Principle:

- <u>Team</u>: All team members understand how to perform their work

<u>Essence Checklist Clarifying Note</u>:

There will always be varying levels of understanding of team members related to how to perform work. It is essential that mechanisms be established to help less experienced workers continuously raise their level of work performance. Working closely with an experienced team member is a proven and practical way to help less experienced workers raise their level of understanding and performance.

<u>Reference Story</u>: Story Four; "Why product specific checklists help performance"

Upside Down Principle Twenty:

 Traditional thinking: Test procedures (or any other procedures) need to be written at the step by step detailed level so that less experienced personnel can use them.

Extended clarifying thought/ Clarifying activities:

It is true that step by step detailed test procedures (or any other procedure) can help to ensure less experienced personnel can apply the procedure correctly (e.g. set up and conduct tests properly). However, trade-offs should be considered balancing the cost of developing and maintaining detailed procedures versus the risk in relying to some degree on the skill level of more experienced personnel.

✔ Essence Checklists Relevant to Principle:

- Way of Working: The capability gaps that exist between what is needed to execute the desired way of working and the capability levels of the team have been analyzed and understood

Essence Checklist Clarifying Note:

When you analyze your capability gaps you will find your capability needs are likely to vary based on your agreed-to way of working. Keep in mind there are often trade-offs to be considered when examining capability needs and the agreed-to way of working, as seen in the regression test procedures Story Four at NORO.

Reference Story: Story Four; Coaching Tip #7

Upside Down Principle Twenty-One:

 Traditional thinking: Sometimes we just don't know enough to break the work down.

👍 **Extended clarifying thought/ Clarifying activities:**

Even when you know you need to do more analysis because you don't know enough about the problem, you can always create completion criteria with a clear definition of done.

✔ # Essence Checklists Relevant to Principle:

- Work: The work is being broken down into actionable work items with clear definition of done
- Team: The team consistently meets its commitments
- Stakeholders: The stakeholder representatives agree with how their different priorities and perspectives are being balanced to provide clear direction to the team

Essence Checklists Clarifying Note:

You can always break your work down to fit in your sprint size, with clear definition of done as demonstrated in story five, coaching tip #14. Also demonstrated in this story is why this is the best way to help your team meet its commitments consistently. This story highlights the importance of making sure the goal and the done criteria are clear and agreed to by both the team and the stakeholders.

It is unrealistic to think you can ever get all your stakeholders to agree. However, you can make sure the goal is clear to both the team and the stakeholders. Keep your stakeholders aware of how you are balancing their different priorities and perspectives to provide clear direction to the team, particularly with respect to the goal and the done criteria.

Reference Story: Story Five; Coaching Tip #14

Upside Down Principle Twenty-Two:

 Traditional thinking: We need to estimate so we will know exactly when we will be done.

👍 Extended clarifying thought/ Clarifying activities:

An estimate is just that. No matter how good our processes or our people are we can never know exactly when we will be done. But estimating has another value besides giving us an idea when we will be done. It helps us achieve the following two checklists:

✔ Essence Checklists Relevant to Principle:

- Way of Working: The team continually tunes their use of the practices and tools
- Work: A credible plan is in place

Essence Checklist Clarifying Note:

When we estimate we break the work down and it causes us to think about the pieces of our work which leads to continual improvement and a credible plan.

Reference Story: Story Six

 Upside Down Principle Twenty-Three:

 Traditional thinking: It is always better to find and fix defects early.

 Extended clarifying thought/ Clarifying activities:

It is better to find defects close in time to when you insert them. Better yet, find them just before you insert them.

 Essence Checklists Relevant to Principle:

- Software System: Defect levels are acceptable to the stakeholders

Essence Checklist Clarifying Note:

Some defects are better never fixed. If this doesn't make sense to you, return to Story Seven for a refresher.

Reference Story: Story Seven; Coaching Tip #16

Upside Down Principle Twenty-Four:

 <u>Traditional thinking</u>: Understand all your requirements before you design.

<u>Extended clarifying thought/ Clarifying activities</u>:

Show your customer the simplest possible solution to their problem before you ask them for more requirements. Then work with your customer to understand the most critical requirements that are missing. Then fix just those issues and show them what you have before you ask them for more requirements.

<u>Clarifying the Extended clarifying thought/ Clarifying activities</u>:

If you don't quite get the point, the old thinking of "understand all your requirements before you design" (which is still a good fundamental) was upside down in the sense that it was interpreted as "ask your customer for all their requirements before you do any work".

Unfortunately this led many organizations into product visions that were far more complicated than what was needed. This often occurred because of a failure in communication early with regard to the real need that was driving the requirements.

A root cause of this failure was often the fact that the customer actually didn't know their requirements, and we weren't doing enough communicating with them concerning what they actually needed. Seeing a demonstration of a product in operation is one way that has been proven to cut through many of these costly miscommunications.

✔ Essence Checklists Relevant to Principle:

- Opportunity: The stakeholders' needs that generate the opportunity have been established
- Software System: The relevant stakeholders agree that the demonstrated architecture is appropriate
- Requirements: Enough of the requirements are addressed for the resulting system to be acceptable to the stakeholders

Essence Checklist Clarifying Note:

Establish the real need that is driving the requirements, before you ask for requirements. One approach that can help ensure you understand the real need is to show your customer the simplest possible solution to their problem before you ask them for more requirements as NORO did in Story Seven. Sometimes when you show someone a solution that is different than what they were thinking, they realize they don't need all the things they thought they needed to solve their problem.

Reference Story: Story Seven; Coaching Tip #17

Upside Down Principle Twenty-Five:

 Traditional thinking: Ensure your schedule identifies all major dependencies.

 Extended clarifying thought/ Clarifying activities:

Rather than focusing on identifying dependencies, focus on eliminating them.

✔ Essence Checklists Relevant to Principle:

- Work: Tasks are consistently completed on time and within their estimates

Essence Checklist Clarifying Note:

To help consistently complete your tasks within their estimates, eliminate dependencies you can't control.

Reference Story: Story Eight; "Upside down policies at Facebook"

Upside Down Principle Twenty-Six:

 <u>Traditional thinking</u>: To work effectively all your team members need to be fully trained in all your organizational practices.

<u>Extended clarifying thought/ Clarifying activities</u>:

Understanding agreed to and committed principles can often help teams achieve the real intent of organizational practices better than the practices themselves.

✔ Essence Checklists Relevant to Principle:

- <u>Way of Working</u>: The principles and constraints are committed to by the team
- <u>Way of Working</u>: The principles and constraints are agreed to by the stakeholders

<u>Reference Story</u>: Story Eight; "The power of principles in guiding developers"

Final Thought

I stated in the introduction that there is a very real problem centering on common misbeliefs related to **"how to"** best achieve many of our well established software engineering guiding principles.

I also stated that I wrote this book because I believe the stories, together with the principles, principle clarifying thoughts, coaching tips and related Essence framework checklists can stimulate deeper reflection and discussion helping you discover your own best "how to" software engineering approaches within your organization.

Just to be clear, in case anyone has miscontrued my main message in this book, I am certainly not in any sense arguing against the need for– or value of– defined repeatable processes (or practices). Rather, I am setting forth in this book the rationale that supports a better path to achieving the goal we all seek. My hope is that you recognize, as I have, the need for more attention on individual and team coaching, and less emphasis on trying to define processes/practices before we know what works.

It is my hope that this book will at least stimulate conversation in your organization leading you to question **"how much"** effort, **"when"** you conduct that effort, as well as **"how you go about"** conducting the effort, associated with many commonly accepted software engineering activities.

Appendix A: Cross-Reference to Coaching Tips

This appendix provides a cross-reference to the 18 coaching tips in the book. The tips are all practical coaching tips I provided to my clients to help them implement the principles more effectively. Some are "traditional" good coaching tips and are referred to as "coaching tip #X", while others are more "upside down" tips and are therefore referred to as "upside down coaching tip #Y".

Coaching tip #1, Story Four: Coaching developers to connect their responsibilities to what they do each day

Coaching tip #2, Story Four: Coaching technical leaders to recognize when they should "do work" and when they should "coach others in doing work".

Coaching tip #3, Story Four: Improving the code review skills of less experienced developers

Coaching tip #4, Story Four: Guiding experienced developers in becoming better coaches

Coaching tip #5, Story Four: Sharing the benefits of code reviews (beyond finding defects) to motivate better performance

Coaching tip #6, Story Four: Guiding developers to recognize situations where they should ask for help

Coaching tip #7, Story Four: Guiding testers in developing and maintaining a regression test suite

Coaching tip #8, Story Four: Guiding your agile/Scrum team in the pros and cons of choosing different sprint lengths

Coaching tip #9, Story Five: Keeping your team aware of how much work they can do in a day

Coaching tip #10, Story Five: Helping your team understand the best work task size, and what to do when they disagree

Coaching tip #11, Story Five: Helping your team reverse the "we're always reacting to fire-drills" culture

Upside down coaching tip #12, Story Five: Another way to help your team reverse the "we're always reacting to fire-drills" culture

Coaching tip #13, Story Five: General principle to keep in mind when coaching your team to plan better

Upside down coaching tip #14, Story Five: Helping your team break "uncertain work" down without wasting their time

Upside down coaching tip #15, Story Six: The value of estimating– beyond knowing when you will be done

Upside down coaching tip #16, Story Seven: When is it really more costly to detect defects, and when should you fix them?

Upside down coaching tip #17, Story Seven: When is the best time to gather requirements?

Upside down coaching tip #18, Story Seven: Reaffirming the best time to find defects

References

1 OMG Essence Specification

http://www.omg.org/spec/Essence/Current[8]

2 McMahon, Paul E., A Thinking Framework to Power Software Development Team Performance, Crosstalk, The Journal of Defense Software Engineering, Jan/Feb 2015

http://www.crosstalkonline.org/

3 McMahon, Paul E., 15 Fundamentals for Higher Performance in Software Development, Appendix D, PEM Systems, 2014

https://leanpub.com/15fundamentals

4 Jacobson, Ivar, Ng Pan-Wei, McMahon, Paul, Spence, Ian, Lidman, Svante, The Essence of Software Engineering: Applying the SEMAT kernel, Addison-Wesley, Jan, 2013

5 Chrissis, Mary Beth, Konrad, Mike, Shrum, Sandy, CMMI for Development: Guidelines for Process Integration and Product Improvement, V1.3, Third Edition, Addison-Wesley, 2011

6 Ambler, Scott, http://www.ambysoft.com/surveys/success2013.html

7 https://en.wikipedia.org/wiki/All_models_are_wrong[9]

8 McMahon, Paul E, CMMI The Agile Way in Constrained and Regulated Environments, Crosstalk, the Journal of Defense Software Engineering, July/August, 2016

---

[8]http://www.omg.org/spec/Essence/Current
[9]https://en.wikipedia.org/wiki/All_models_are_wrong

http://www.crosstalkonline.org/

9 Scrum Guide, The Definitive Rules of Scrum

http://www.scrumguides.org/docs/

scrumguide/v1/scrum-guide-us.pdf

10 Beck, Kent, Agile Africa, 2015, Keynote Address

https://www.youtube.com/watch?v=I3tTCuhO6ho[10]

11 Ambler, Scott, Lines, Mark, Disciplined Agile Delivery: A Practitioner's Guide to Agile Software Delivery in the Enterprise, IBM Press, June 2012

12 SEMAT Website

http://www.semat.org/

---

[10]https://www.youtube.com/watch?v=I3tTCuhO6ho

About the Author

 Paul E. McMahon (pemcmahon@acm.org, www.pemsystems.com), Principal, PEM Systems has been an independent consultant since 1997 helping organizations increase agility and process maturity. He has taught software engineering at Binghamton University, conducted workshops on engineering processes and management and has published more than 50 articles and multiple books including *Integrating CMMI and Agile Development: Case Studies and Proven Techniques for Faster Performance Improvement,* and *15 Fundamentals for Higher Performance in Software Development.* Paul is a co-author of *The Essence of Software Engineering: Applying the SEMAT Kernel.* Paul is a Certified Scrum Master and a Certified Lean Six Sigma Black Belt. His insights reflect 24 years of experience working for companies such as Link Simulation and Lockheed Martin, and 19 years of consulting/coaching experience. Paul has been a leader in the SEMAT initiative since its initial meeting in Zurich.